SHORT WALK

Lancashire Pubs

Alan Shepley

COUNTRYSIDE BOOKS

NEWBURY, BERKSHIRE

First published 1997
© Alan Shepley 1997

COUNTRYSIDE BOOKS
3 Catherine Road
Newbury, Berkshire

ISBN 1 85306 473 4

Designed by Mon Mohan
Cover illustration by Colin Doggett
Maps and photographs by the author

Produced through MRM Associates Ltd., Reading
Printed by Woolnough Bookbinding Ltd., Irthlingborough

Contents

Introduction   6

Walk   1   Silverdale: The Silverdale Hotel (3½ miles*)   8

       2   Whittington: The Dragons Head (2½ miles)   13

       3   Heysham: The Old Hall Inn (2 miles)   17

       4   Skippool: The River Wyre (4 miles*)   21

       5   Wrea Green: The Grapes (3½ miles*)   26

       6   Woodplumpton: The Wheatsheaf (2½ miles*)   30

       7   Whitewell: The Inn at Whitewell (1½ miles)   35

       8   Slaidburn: The Hark to Bounty Inn (2½ miles*)   40

       9   Tosside: The Dog and Partridge (2½ miles)   44

      10   Halsall: The Saracens Head (1½ miles)   49

      11   Rufford: The Hesketh Arms (1½ miles)   54

      12   Leyland: The Eagle and Child (2¼ miles)   58

      13   Astley Village (Chorley): The Barons Rest
           (1½ miles)   63

      14   Hoghton: The Boars Head (3 ½ miles*)   67

      15   Clitheroe: The Bridge (3 miles*)   71

      16   Salterforth: The Anchor Inn (2½ miles)   76

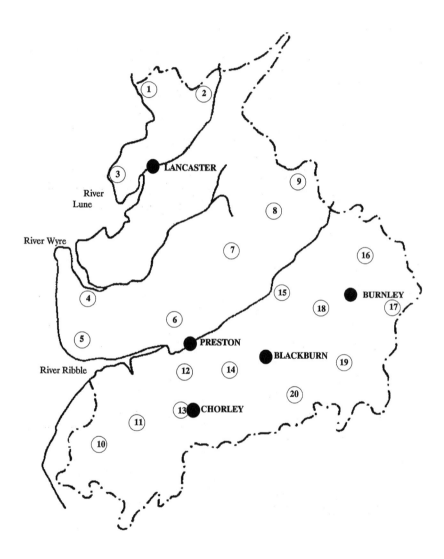

Area map showing locations of the walks.

17   Wycoller: The Herders Inn (2½ miles)   80

18   Habergham Eaves: The George IV (4 miles*)   84

19   Haslingden Grane: The Holden Arms (3 miles*) 88

20   Entwistle: The Strawbury Duck (3 miles)   93

* Shorter circuits are also described.

Key to Sketch Maps

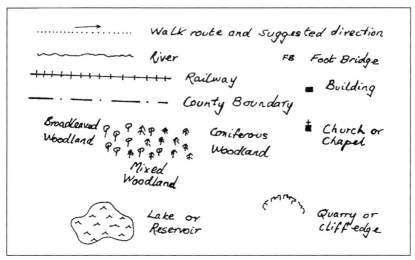

Publisher's Note

We hope that you obtain considerable enjoyment from this book; great care has been taken in its preparation. However, changes of landlord and actual closures are sadly not uncommon. Likewise, although at the time of publication all routes followed public rights of way or permitted paths, diversion orders can be made and permissions withdrawn.

We cannot of course be held responsible for such diversion orders and any inaccuracies in the text which result from these or any other changes to the routes nor any damage which might result from walkers trespassing on private property. We are anxious though that all details covering the walks and the pubs are kept up to date and would therefore welcome information from readers which would be relevant to future editions.

Introduction

Compiling a further guide to pub walks in Lancashire (see also *Pub Walks in Lancashire*) has provided several extra opportunities. Perhaps the most pleasurable has been the chance to include some well worthwhile locations that there was simply no room for in the previous volume, especially those delightful spots which are (perhaps too often) thought of as 'town' as distinct from 'country'. In addition, the emphasis has been moved to shorter – and, usually, easier – routes. A greater proportion of the pubs themselves is suited to the younger family or the walk is linked to other attractions which will enhance your day out with the family.

Though I have spent most of my life walking the paths and byways of the county, I find myself as enthusiastic as ever for the scenery, wildlife and history of the Lancashire countryside. Despite all efforts to make it otherwise, it remains one of England's most attractive and varied counties.

Once again, there have been changes in local government administration boundaries whilst this book was in preparation. The area covered is that of other volumes (see *Lancashire Rambles*, and *Walks for Motorists: Lancashire*). Only time will tell whether the changes make any significant difference to public usage of rights of way.

Each of the walks in this book is circular and is illustrated by a sketch map, designed to guide you to the starting point and give you a simple yet accurate idea of the route to be taken. However, I still strongly recommend that you take a copy of the Ordnance Survey 1:50 000 scale map (Landranger) with you. This is very helpful for identifying the main features of views, remember that perfectly legitimate changes may have taken place on the ground since I last passed through.

A word of caution with regard to dogs: farm stock and domestic pets do not on the whole, mix – please remember that it is your dog which is the visitor and that public rights extend to the right of way only, and not to the surrounding land. The countryside is, after all, a workplace for many.

Distances are indicated, but times for each walk will depend on the weather and the membership of the party. All the walks are quite safe and straightforward, but where a potential hazard presents itself, for example because of tides or old quarry workings, this is mentioned in the walk description. Footwear with a good grip is a wise investment to cope with the general hazards of muddy ground, wet rocks, slippy grass and so on, and even on short walks, the British climate can change quickly so being prepared for rain is a sensible precaution.

As a matter of policy this book has been compiled in accordance with the guidance for writers of path guides produced by the Outdoor Writers' Guild and each walk has been revisited during its preparation. If, however, readers do find any changes on the ground that would be relevant to future editions, the publisher would be pleased to hear from them. Even more likely than changes in walk details are changes in the pub offerings. The information given is as accurate as possible at the time of writing but a particular landlord is not a permanent fixture and policies on menus, opening hours, and facilities for children can alter quite often for a variety of reasons. Similarly, most pubs are happy for you to leave your car in their car park whilst you do the walk, but please ask permission first. Telephone numbers are given so that you can phone ahead and check details.

The majority of pubs included can be reached by public transport as well as by car. Some of you will, I know, prefer this option anyway. Sadly, timetables are probably the most changeable feature of all and details would be rapidly out of date. A look at the Yellow Pages should enable you to find current information direct from the service providers or from the Tourist Information Centres.

It is my pleasure, finally, to thank all those who have helped in the preparation of this book. Many have done so as I have walked around the county, and many are my long-gone predecessors who have written with enthusiasm in a host of books and articles which have helped me enjoy my walking over the years. I remain firmly of the belief that the more who come to know and enjoy the land through the pleasure of walking it themselves, the more of it we shall pass on enhanced (or, at least, unsullied) to future generations to enjoy in their turn.

Alan Shepley

① Silverdale
The Silverdale Hotel

The area between the rivers Kent and Keer forms a peninsula which is unique in landscape and wildlife interest (most of it is designated as an Area of Outstanding Natural Beauty). Over half the area lies within Lancashire and its present-day focus is at Silverdale. In the past, when travel was made difficult by the marshes and the high tides, the centres of population were in villages like Warton and the Yealands. Until the railway came it must have been a very inward-looking community and, even today, it has a detached air about it.

The Silverdale Hotel stands beside the Shore Road. A listed building, it began life as the Britannia before 1836 and was an assembly point for travellers crossing the Sands. It has been a favourite haunt of many down the years including such well-known authors as Mrs Gaskell and J.B. Priestley. They would, I guess, have been entirely happy with the tasteful modernisation.

Food is available all day during the summer and at weekends in the winter; weekday winter service is from 12 noon to 3 pm and from 6 pm to 9 pm. The bar menu is extensive and is supplemented by salads, sandwiches and filled jacket potatoes. A local flavour to things is always welcome so Silverdale chicken (in a mushroom, courgette and tomato casserole), preceded by home-made pâté, and followed with the daily offering of fruit sorbet should get the taste-buds going. There is a vegetarian choice and the children are catered for too. This is a freehouse open from 11 am to 11 pm (10.30 pm on Sundays). Beers are Whitbread Best, Boddingtons Bitter, Marston's Pedigree and Flowers IPA. Lagers are Heineken and Stella Artois, stout both Guinness and Murphy's and the cider is Strongbow. Families are welcome and will find a non-smoking area and family area inside. The garden is delightful and it gives space in which the children can play. Please check before taking your dog beyond the garden.

Telephone: 01524 701206. Accommodation is available.

How to get there: From the north, leave the A6 at Milnthorpe on the B2582 and follow any of the signs for Silverdale; turn at the sign for the shore. From the south, leave the A6 at Carnforth and pass the station on the road for Warton; turn at the sign for Silverdale and, in the village, take the turning for the shore.

Parking: There is a large car park adjacent to the hotel. In addition, public parking exists at The Cove, in the village centre and on the shore itself.

Length of the walk: 3½ miles, or 3 miles if you return direct from the church. Map: OS Landranger sheet 97 Kendal and Morecambe (inn GR 459748).

The route is an easy one with only minor rises and falls and includes the shore and mixed woodland as well as pleasant views.

The Walk

Note: Some of the channels on the shore are deep and fast-flowing so when the tide is in it may be necessary to use the alternative approach to The Cove. Wandering further out onto the Sands is dangerous and should not be attempted.

Turn right from the hotel entrance and descend Shore Road, past a farmhouse on the left dated 1744. The car park notice at the shore

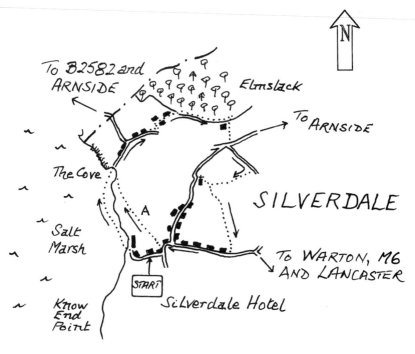

itself makes clear the dangers of the tide. (If the tide is in opt for the alternative route described below.) Move out a little and walk right with Grange over Sands nestling low on the far side of the Kent estuary and the Lakeland Fells beyond. You should be able to find a rough track over the saltmarsh. Follow this as best you may, with deviations to find points at which the channels may be crossed (sometimes a jump rather than a stride) and work along parallel to the low cliffs until more or less opposite a very obvious cove with a man-made 'cave' in the limestone cliff on its far side. Turn in and rejoin the land.

The alternative route, 'A' on the sketch map, crosses the fields called The Lots from the steps and gate just 50 yards east of the hotel. Follow through the wood to The Cove, where there is a reserve sign.

Walk up the lane past Cove Cottage and turn right at the road junction. Use the footway and cross over to the footpath at the postbox. Turn left away from the road between limestone walls. At the surfaced lane, continue ahead across the zig-zag on the footpath

Limestone cliffs at The Cove.

for Elmslack, past Windyridge. Go between large houses and eventually through a garden and via a tunnel of overgrowth into Wallings Lane. At the end, go left and right by the Castlebank sign and enter Eaves Wood.

Continue along the wood, by a track between walls, to pass a tall gate on the right marked 'private'. One hundred yards on, between a large yew and an ash, bear sharply down to the right (there is no sign). Descend the right-hand boundary of a field, with a wire fence on your left, and reach the road beside the entrance to the Woodlands Hotel, opposite Bottoms Lane.

Walk along Bottoms Lane to the end of the first field and take the footpath right. Keep the left-hand wall of the same field close and aim towards the church. The path goes left through a white gate and takes the same line to a squeeze stile behind houses. At the junction of tracks cross into St John's churchyard. This building was not consecrated until 1886, but it is the latest in a long succession which goes back, at least, to before 1100. The relative opulence of the building, and the memorials in it, speak of the incoming wealth of Victorian Silverdale.

For the shorter walk, exit to the road and turn left to follow it through the village, but you will miss a splendid view.

For the main walk, return behind the church, then bear round right to the path for Stankelt Road and enter fields. Away to the left is the edge of the Yorkshire Dales. Follow the right-hand boundary to a green lane beside a house and pass a brick barn and exit to Stankelt Road. Follow the footway easily down and bear left at the junction for the shore to return to the hotel.

Places of interest nearby
Close by are three reserves on *Warton Crag*, and the internationally famous RSPB reserve of *Leighton Moss* (beside Silverdale station) which has displays and public viewing hides both on the Moss and Morecambe Bay. The *Wolfhouse Gallery* is an especially popular craft centre, and *Leighton Hall* is open to view and has a bird of prey centre.

② Whittington
The Dragons Head

The sandstone cottages and houses of Whittington village straddle a bend in the minor road on the western side of the middle reaches of the Lune valley. The unusual pub name relates to the coat of arms of the North family of the nearby Newton Hall (not, surprisingly, the Greens of nearer Whittington Hall). Built as a country residence by Squire Burrow over 150 years ago, the Dragons Head has been a pub since 1900. Today it also serves as the village post office. The barn beside the car park was once a coach house and the cottage next door is still known as Coachman's Cottage.

Food is served at lunchtime (12 noon to 2.30 pm) and in the evening (6 pm to 9 pm) each day, with a slightly extended evening menu. The range is a reasonable one, in any case; since we are in fishing country, my own choice would be baked trout after a simple soup starter and with Lancashire apple pie to follow. Lighter eaters will find sandwiches and salads available too. There are vegetarian and children's choices. This is a Mitchell's house and serves their own Original as well as guest beers. Bar times are 11 am to 11 pm

(10.30 pm on Sunday). Stout is Guinness and lager Carlsberg. The cider is Strongbow. An area for families is set aside in the pool room; there is no play area (though they do have boules!) but there is a playground at the end of the village (see the walk description below). The beer garden has a pleasant outlook and you may eat your own food here. Please ask before taking your dog into the building.

Telephone: 01524 272383. Accommodation is available.

How to get there: The pub is in the centre of the village on the B6254. Turn from the A65 at Kirkby Lonsdale, or from the A6 in Carnforth centre.

Parking: Behind the pub, but please ask before leaving your car there while you walk.

Length of the walk: 2½ miles. Map: OS Landranger sheet 97 Kendal and Morecambe (inn GR 601760).

The walk is almost flat and very easy going underfoot, with extensive views of the middle Lune valley and considerable wildlife interest in the area of the river. The attractive village has several old cottages.

The Walk
Turn left from the pub door and follow the narrow cobbled footway along the village street; across the road a decorated cottage door is dated 1687. Pass the sandstone terrace and continue on along the verge to the bend and the farm of Low Hall. Take the bridleway to the left and immediately pass the tennis courts and a children's playground. Views open out straight away across the valley to the Forest of Bowland and up the valley to Ingleborough. The firm, straight track between hedges is Burrow Mill Lane and passes a small sewage plant screened by pines and then does a double right angle. In the hedges either side you will see some point-to-point jumps. The course is used by the Vale of Lune Hunt and Holcombe Harriers around Easter each year, and for other races too (the pub will be able to tell you when races are on) – the village is packed with visitors then.

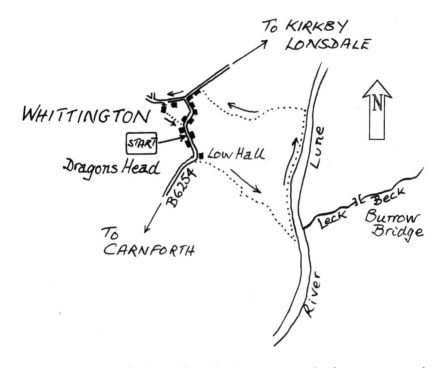

When you reach the cattle grid, aim across to the far gatepost and oak tree and join the river bank more or less opposite the point at which the Leck Beck joins the Lune. There was once a ford to where the modern bungalow stands on the far bank; it is no longer, sadly, practicable to use it. Up to the left you can make out the Georgian Burrow Hall and, in the field in front of it, the hummocky remains of a Roman camp. Walk upstream, with the view up the valley beyond Barbon to the Yorkshire Dales beyond, and of the village church clear on a rise to your left. Pass a fisherman's hut and two stiles and continue by the river with a wooded bank in the field to your left. A variety of waterfowl, especially duck, inhabit the river at all seasons, and oystercatchers nest on the shingle banks. Go ahead over a further stile and then left at the next one almost opposite a shingle bank and near an old green caravan. Use the gate in the corner and head direct for the church tower. Go between hedges to a gate by the farm bridge and then use the farm track; on your right is an interesting exposure of the boulder-filled soil of the valley. The village ahead is backed by West

Middle Lune valley.

Hall Park wood and it should be possible to make out Whittington Hall, just beyond the church. At the 'private' sign follow the arrow right and walk up the old track by the left-hand boundary of the field and go right at the gate onto a concrete track to the main road just right of the houses.

Cross over, with care for the traffic, and walk left past the haulage yard into the village. Take the right turn, signed for Sellet Hall Herb Gardens (perhaps also worth a visit while you are in the area), then use the footway on the left past St Michael's Manor House (1650) and go up the steps to the church and round to the west doorway. The tower is of the 1500s and the font is old, but most of St Michael's was rebuilt in 1875. When you have had a look round, leave the churchyard down the steps to the squeeze stile below the cedar trees and walk along the left-hand boundary through the green iron gate and the white kissing-gate (the view back to the church on the brow is an excellent one). Follow the path over the field to a ginnel which reaches the road again by the old school (1875). Turn right past the village hall and cross back to the pub.

③ Heysham
The Old Hall Inn

Like a pearl, Heysham lies hidden between the visually unattractive power station and port and the straggling suburbs of Morecambe. Like a pearl, it is well worth seeking out for here lies a unique piece of coastline and some fascinating history.

The Old Hall Inn is exactly what its name implies – the old hall of Higher Heysham. Medieval owners of the manor were bound to meet the king at the Lancashire boundary with a horn and white staff, to attend on him during his stay in the county and to see him safely on his way afterwards. The exterior of the building is essentially as it was built in about 1598. The interior suffered many alterations down the years – including secret passages through the massive chimneys – but was restored in keeping by the brewery when it was converted into a pub in the late 1950s (notice the specially designed carpet based on Queen Elizabeth I's Bible). Quite unusually, the pub also serves as the local Tourist Information Centre.

Food service is from 11 am to 2.30 pm and between 5.30 pm and

7.30 pm (12 noon to 7.30 pm on Sundays). There is, of course, a specials board each day but a prawn cocktail starter will make you think, at least, of Morecambe Bay, and the Cumberland sausage with cranberry sauce is redolent of the fells across the Sands. Sunday sees a special menu with roast beef (they do a children's serving of this) and the pie of the day is extremely popular. Sandwiches and jacket potatoes are also served. There is a separate menu for children. This is a Mitchell's pub with their famous Lancaster Bomber beer, Tetley Mild and Original and guest beers. Castlemaine and Carlsberg are the lagers, Strongbow the cider and the stout is Guinness. There is a good selection of whiskies and English country wines. Bar times are 11 am to 11 pm (10.30 pm on Sunday). Families will feel at home here and will find an excellent play area beside the beer garden. You are welcome to consume your own food in the garden where your dog may also relax.

Telephone: 01524 851209.

How to get there: Either approach along the A5105 from Morecambe and look for the pub set back to your right, or use the A589 from Lancaster and turn left on the new road signed for Heysham port through White Lund Industrial Estate, opposite the college; go right at the port roundabout and find the pub set back to the left.

Parking: There is a large car park at the pub.

Length of the walk: 2 miles. Map: OS Landranger sheet 97 Kendal and Morecambe (inn GR 415611).

Heysham Head is of a reddish sandstone and the first rocky headland north of the Welsh border. On it stand the remains of rock graves and a chapel and the church close by is equally fascinating. The old village centre and fishing cove might well be in Cornwall, not Lancashire. The walk is easy and an alternative route is available for use when the tide is in.

The Walk
Cross to the right of the car park and go over School Road in front of Towers Cottages. Use the footway past Beech Stores on the left, then take the third right into Smithy Lane and walk up over the

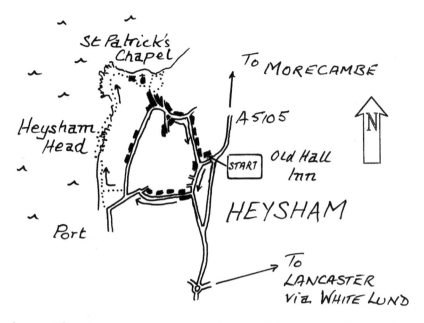

brow. The view opens immediately over Morecambe Bay and, as you drop down, the nuclear power station (with a Visitor Centre – telephone: 015324 855624) and port are just round to the left. At the T-junction at the bottom you may either go left and right on the shore at the sign, or go right for 20 yards then through the fence to the left and along the wall to reach the shore over the grassy area. If the tide is suitable, make your way carefully amongst the rocks round the first headland and edge up right amongst the grass and gorse, blackberry and honeysuckle to St Patrick's chapel on the hill (this area is now National Trust). If the tide is against you, you will have to walk along the road from the junction into the village centre and bear down left to reach the chapel from the other side.

The chapel is a simple rectangle and may have stood, overlooking Half Moon Bay, since the 8th century. Immediately beside it is a series of rock-hewn graves lying east-west; one is child-size. If you can watch the sunset from this point I have no doubt that you will find no difficulty in imagining yourself back with our ancestors! Drop down from the chapel to the adjacent St Peter's church (there is a sheltered picnic site just behind the high wall to the right). This only looks younger because it has been restored over the years. Parts of it are Saxon and beside the path is a Saxon cross. Inside are

Rock-cut graves at Heysham Head.

a hogsback tombstone and the tomb of a Crusader. Beside the churchyard is the Glebe garden – a quiet oasis created and looked after by local people.

Exit from the churchyard and bear down left. Look at Yew Tree Cottage (1681) and the garden of the old rectory, Greese House (1680). Take Main Street to the tiny boat launch on the bay. Return to the corner, then go left on Bailey Street and continue 50 yards past the footpath which leads to Morecambe promenade. Turn to the right past Carr Garth and follow the blue pedestrian sign for the church and shops through the ginnel with the steps and rail, then turn left in front of the old Royal Hotel (a ship, not a king). Even older cottages (1629 and 1633) lie either side of the street.

The large central square has shops, and cafés (selling the famous Heysham nettle beer), toilets and a massive car park. Walk up to the left by Rookery View and the stone cottages – the view is, in fact, across to the wooded back of the headland on which you stood earlier. Bear back up left before the terrace of Carr Lane/Lees Court and go right on the footway up Longlands Lane. In 100 yards, go right along School Lane, pass the school and return to the pub.

4 Skippool
The River Wyre

The estuary of the Wyre winds a considerable distance inland. Just to the west of the lowest crossing, at Shard Bridge (this newest bridge was only put up in 1992), is the backwater of Skippool. Once upon a time this was a mini-port for wine, rum, sugar, tobacco, and flax bound for the mills at Kirkham, but Fleetwood and the motor-car have passed it by and many will drive through without even knowing it is there. The River Wyre (claimed to be the only pub in England called after a river) was purpose-built in 1896 with the hope of cashing in on the sea trade (Poulton had its own customs house then). Even King Edward VII is reputed to have called in on one occasion.

The River Wyre was fully refurbished in 1996 and presents a bright and welcoming interior to the visitor. Food is available every day from 12 noon to 10 pm. What the menu refers to as 'fork and pitcher' pies are hearty fillers for a cold winter's day and the other main courses are a taste of old England – the roast meats are very popular. Starters include that wonderful invention the potato skin –

filled here with bacon and cheese – this might win the prize for the finest addition to pub menus of recent years. The salads are an unusually wide selection and you can push the humble sandwich to a triple-decker! Vegetarian choice is good and children are catered for. The bar is open all day from 11 am to 11 pm (12 noon to 10.30 pm on Sundays). A Bass house, their bitter and mild, Worthington ale and Caffrey's are carried as well as guest beers. The lager is the infrequently met Staropramen, stout is Guinness and the cider is Blackthorn. There is a good range of old malt whisky. Inside you will find a non-smoking area and outside a beer garden. Dogs are not permitted in the bars.

Telephone: 01253 883791.

How to get there: Use the A585 from the Blackpool or Preston/Lancaster sides; the pub stands at the roundabout where the A588 joins from Poulton le Fylde centre and the B5412 joins from Thornton.

Parking: There is a substantial pub car park and parking on the old road in front of it.

Length of the walk: 4 miles (1½ miles on the shorter, alternative route). Map: OS Landranger sheet 102 Preston and Blackpool (inn GR 355405).

The full walk is the longest in this collection but it is easy and flat; the shorter, alternative circuit precludes visiting the marvellous Stanah Country Park but is recommended as a 'taster' at times when the highest tides flood the estuary edge. The outward quiet and leafy lanes contrast with the wide skies, running tide and the birds and flora of the estuary with its leisure boating.

The Walk

Cross over the A585 from the front of the pub with some care; immediately over the fence is the head of Skippool Creek itself. Bear left along the footway of the B5412 and go past the Thornton Lodge and the strangely castellated building of Illawalla to Thornton Hall on the bend of the road – beware of the very narrow section of footway here. Continue past the first houses and take the path to the right across the field. At the stile on the far side you come to a lane.

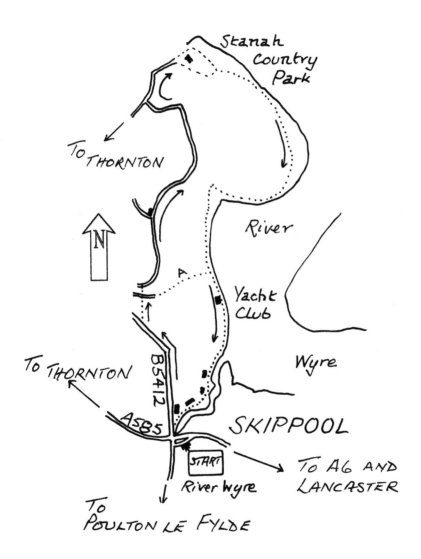

Stanah
Country
Park

To Thornton

N

River

To Thornton

B5412

A

Yacht
Club

Wyre

A585

SKIPPOOL

START

River Wyre

To A6 and
Lancaster

To
Poulton le Fylde

The river Wyre.

The short, alternative route ('A' on the map) turns right along the lane here and goes directly down to the shore – see below for the continuation from that point. At times of high tide this route is recommended.

For the main route, go over the lane, cross a second field, exit onto Raikes Road and turn to the right. Follow the lane with a low ridge in the fields to the right cutting off the view to the estuary. Take the right fork at the cottage along Underbank Road to pass Nestleton and eventually reach Stanah farm with its cobbled barns. Continue along Stanah Road and go right along River Road. The Archimedes' screws of the pumping station can be seen on the left. Enter the country park, with the ICI Hillhouse site next door – originally based on the pumping of brine from rock salt beds deep below. There is a Countryside Service Information Centre here and an educational ecology centre. A wide variety of leaflets and booklets are on sale. The park site was created in 1989 from a rubbish-tip on the marsh. The view seaward extends to Fleetwood and Knott End, on the other bank, and the Lakeland Fells in the far distance. The park is a good place for birdwatching. Large flocks of waders and wildfowl feed on the estuary; herons, cormorants, gulls, a variety of finches, and the smaller hawks are common. The far side of the estuary is a large saltmarsh and small areas, with their peculiar flora, exist on this side too.

Leave the park by walking upstream along the shore and join the stoned path which wanders along up the estuary. Notice the safety sign about the tides and quicksands; at very high tides the path gets covered over and you should always be prepared for mud here. Before you is the view up towards the Bowland Fells and across the water is the village of Hambleton. Continue past the small picnic area at Cockle Hall (now demolished), skirt the shore and swing round into the embayment of Ramper Pot. Stay with the shore and go past the long series of rather ramshackle jetties for the moored leisure boats. Further along the path the alternative route rejoins the shore.

Walk through the Blackpool and Fleetwood Yacht Club and over the slipway. Shard Bridge is visible upriver. Continue along the track past the restaurant and the picnic site on the right and exit in front of a row of houses and the Thornton Lodge. Recross the main road to the River Wyre.

Places of interest nearby
Close by is the fine museum in the rebuilt *Marsh Mill in Wyre* (telephone: 01253 860765, GR 336431), in Thornton, with an excellent explanation of the history of the mill, how it works, and the immediate surroundings. The cap and sails are complete and work on occasion. It is open to visitors throughout the year.

⑤ Wrea Green
The Grapes

The folk of Wrea Green are very proud of their community – others must get heartily fed-up with their success in keeping the village so attractive and winning prizes for it over such a long period of time. To say that it has merely 'chocolate box' attractiveness is to miss the genuine way in which the green itself, thatched cottages, the church and its spire and the pub complement each other. The summer evening shadows as a cricket match draws to a close are a delight. Other villages may vie with Wrea Green, but few can surpass it. The Grapes has been beside the green a long time; parts of the building go back to the 1600s. Once upon a time it rejoiced in the name of the Dumpling. Recent refurbishment and updating has been well done and it is an attractive and welcoming place.

Food is served from 12 noon to 2.30 pm and 5 pm to 10 pm on weekdays, and all day at the weekend, from 12 noon to 10 pm. The menu of 'Henry's Table' is a very extensive one with low-fat encouragements for weight-watchers and many vegetarian options; there's even the fun of cooking your own meat on a grillstone at your table. My own choice would be from amongst the English meat dishes, but there are some interesting exotic meals too. Children's portions are available. A Greenalls house, the beers are Boddingtons and Flowers plus guest beers. Lagers are Heineken, Stella Artois, and Labatts while the stouts are Guinness and Murphy's and the lighter Caffrey's. Cider is Strongbow. The bar opens at 11 am and service is all day to 11 pm (12 noon to 10.30 pm on Sundays). A pleasant patio between the pub and the green serves as a beer garden, and the green itself is a fine play area for the children. Please note that dogs are not allowed inside the pub.

Telephone: 01772 682927.

How to get there: Turn from the A583 Preston to Blackpool road onto the B5259 or the B5260. The Grapes is at the junction of the two B roads.

Parking: At the pub and around the green. Please ask before leaving your car in the pub car park while you walk.

Length of the walk: 3½ miles; a minimum would be a wander round the green – less than ½ mile; a shortening of the route is to return from the entrance to Ribby Leisure Village – 2 miles; an extension is to go into the centre of Kirkham on foot – 2 miles extra. Map: OS Landranger sheet 102 Preston and Blackpool (inn GR 397315).

A pleasant, flat walk, flexible in length, mainly through fields and beside woods, much of it on track or lane. The village green deserves a circuit for its thatched cottages and the remains of the former windmill. An optional extension to Kirkham reveals some remaining Georgian brick houses and the church with its tall Victorian steeple.

The Walk

At the very least, it is well worth while walking around the green itself. Immediately beside the pub is St Nicholas' church, built in 1849 by an architect who knew exactly how high the spire should be to fit the view from across the green. This apparently unchanging, grassy sward and its duck pond became the village's own property only as recently as 1972. Tucked down one of the

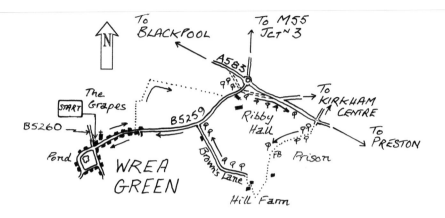

side roads off the green are the remains of the old windmill, now a house. The best of the thatched cottages are just across from the church.

   Leave the green in the direction of Kirkham and use the footway to a path on the left just before the mini-roundabout; several of the houses along this stretch have fine doorways and windows. The start looks like the entrance to Highgate Cottage only but look carefully and you will see the stile set back about 20 yards. Walk ahead along a hedged track between the fields and beneath some fine ash trees. The track dog-legs behind the children's playground and under a telephone line. Bear round to the right between overgrown hedges rich with oak, elder, alder, willow, hazel and gorse and with small blue butterflies flitting amongst the vegetation in summertime. The path passes an old gritstone pillar as you cross four stiles to the Ribby road which you reach just along from the entrance to the Ribby Leisure Village. (It is possible to shorten the route by returning along the footway to the right from this point.)

   Cross over the road with a care for traffic and walk to the left past the old stables and beside the wall of the former estate of the Hornbys of Ribby Hall. Parishes in this part of the county are often linked and, even today, this remains Ribby-with-Wrea. The hall itself is late Georgian but not visible from the route. Follow the sandstone estate wall tightly round to the right beside the main Preston road. Over the wall is substantial woodland of sycamore with many hollies beneath. Walk along the verge to pass the layby and turn to the right on Powater Road. (It is possible to divert into

Thatched cottages beside the Green.

the centre of old Kirkham – once the site of a Roman fort – from this point by crossing over the A583.)

At the end, facing you, is gate 22 in the perimeter fence of Kirkham Open Prison. Take the stile to the right before it and enter a wood over a further stile. Keep to the left-hand path and find a footbridge over a ditch and stile at the corner of a caravan site (you are now at the far corner of Ribby Hall park). Enter the field and follow the right-hand boundary up the rise to a stile just right of the modern barn. Continue ahead past the new house of Windrush Stud farm to your left and bear slightly right to reach the track just below Hill Farm. Walk between the farm buildings to join Brown's Lane and follow this round the edge of the hall estate. The woodland edge and the field hedges here often seem especially full of flocks of finches. Far to the left are the West Pennine Moors and the tall gas holder of Southport is clearly visible nearer at hand. Continue past Woodside Cottage and Brown's Farm to the main road. Cross to the footway and walk back into the village.

6 Woodplumpton
The Wheatsheaf

These days the M55 forms a firm boundary to the northward spread of urban Preston. The mainly grazing land on the well-drained soils beyond it is a patchwork of small fields with hundreds of ponds still dotting the landscape. The village of Woodplumpton straggles beside the road, with the old ford of the brook to the south, the church at the top of the rise and the Wheatsheaf, at the road side, just around the bend beyond. Its low ceilings give the pub a cosy feel which, no doubt, has been a constant since it was built in 1767.

Food is available every lunchtime throughout the week from 12 noon to 2 pm. The range is simple and straightforward and includes a popular home-made steak pie and good soup. If a snack is all you require there are also sandwiches, salads and burgers. On weekdays the bar times are 11.30 am to 2.30 pm and 6 pm to 11 pm, on Saturdays they are 11 am to 3 pm and 7 pm to 11 pm, while Sunday times are 12 noon to 4.30 pm and 7 pm to 10.30 pm. As a Scottish Courage house Theakston Best Bitter and Mild, and Marston's

Pedigree and a guest beer are on draught. The lagers are Harp, Slalom and McEwans Extra, while the stout is Guinness and the cider is Strongbow. There is a small but pleasant beer garden. Please ask before taking your dog into the pub.

Telephone: 01772 690301.

How to get there: Approach from Preston town centre on the B5411 via Ingol, or use the B5269 from the A6 at Broughton and turn off at the sign for Woodplumpton. The Wheatsheaf is at the south end of the village.

Parking: At the pub and on the side road close by. Please ask before leaving your car in the pub car park while you walk.

Length of the walk: 2½ miles, or a shorter circuit of just ¾ mile. Map: OS Landranger sheet 102 Preston and Blackpool (inn GR 500344).

A pleasant, undulating walk through fields and by the canal. Woodplumpton church is outstanding as a building. The grave of Old Meg the witch is an interesting curiosity for children of all ages. A short route is available.

The Walk

Cross the road from the pub door and walk left to enter the churchyard of St Anne's. The outside of the building is best viewed from the far end. A south aisle was added in 1748 and contrasts with the 12th-century north aisle; the little tower joins them in an outstandingly attractive harmony. There appear to be three sundials of various sorts on the building – see if you can find them. The site has certainly been occupied by a church since at least Norman times. Close to the south-west corner of the church is a glacial erratic boulder beneath which, it is said, lies the grave of the witch Old Meg Shelton. It was she who was reputed to have milked dry the fabulous milk cow of Grimsargh, near Longridge, amongst the many evil tricks she played on the locals of the area. Why, when she died, she ever came to be buried within the consecrated ground of the churchyard is something of a mystery but putting the boulder over her was a sensible precaution to prevent her escaping. At the sound of the midnight bell the boulder itself is reliably reported to rotate!

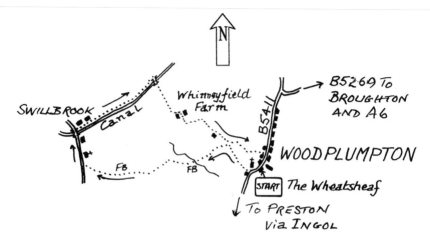

Leave the witch's grave and exit from the churchyard by the stile in the north wall. Follow the right-hand hedge to a gate to a metalled lane.

The short circuit is to go through the gate and turn to the right, then follow the directions in the final paragraph.

To continue the main walk, turn left at a right angle in front of the gate and cross the field to the gap on the far side by the ash tree. Just beyond it is a duck-filled pond overhung by trees. Skirt this on the right and, at the far end, bear half-right and drop down under the power line to a footbridge over the Woodplumpton Brook. Turn to the right-hand hedge and cross the boundary beside the brook. Walk diagonally half-right to a gate by a small pond filled with yellow flag in season (a heron lazily flapped away as I passed). Go ahead and cross the field to a bar stile beside an oak in the hedge and bear right on the far side to a footbridge in the corner. Follow the right-hand boundary via a stile and reach a lane at a steel gate beside the modern Crown Lane Free Methodist church, opposite Rosemary Lane. Walk to the right along the verge for 250 yards, ignoring the footpath right, and reach the bridge over the Lancaster Canal beside Swillbrook House. Over the parapet, to the left, is the milestone which records 8 miles from Preston.

Cross the bridge and turn right on the towpath through Catforth Boat Hire and Sales, which occupies the old canal cottages and stables for the horses which used to pull the barges. This is always an active spot and a variety of craft will be seen. As you walk north,

St Anne's church.

the view opens up to the fells of the Forest of Bowland, the almost separate Parlick standing out. The canal has the usual moorhens, coots and ducks and the occasional swan; summertime sees swallows hawking for insects over the water beside the tall grasses and yellow flag, with cow parsley and angelica lining the hedgerow. In a short distance you cross back over the Woodplumpton Brook on a short, and uninteresting, aqueduct and then come to Whinneyfield bridge (no 34).

Turn up and over the bridge, using the steps, and follow the track to a steel gate, then head left for the black and white farmhouse of Whinneyfield. Go right at its near end, between the house and the barn, and join the access lane. The pink variety of hawthorn blossoms in the hedge here. Walk easily along past Whinny Cottage farm and come to the other side of the steel gate you were at earlier, here joining the route of the short-cut.

Continue ahead and reach the main village street by the school. Turn right. On the school wall a plaque records that this was 'Preston Guild Village in 1992' – a rare honour, since the Preston Guild celebrations only take place every 21 years. Return across the road to the pub.

A typical waymark post.

Places of interest nearby
Close by, just off the B5269 Broughton to Longridge road, is Chingle Hall. Built in 1260, it is one of the few moated houses in the country where the moat still survives. It is said to be haunted by the ghost of St John Wall, a Catholic born there in 1620. He was sent to France to be educated as a missionary priest and was martyred at Worcester in 1679. His friends reputedly took his head to France and then returned it to the Hall at the time of the Revolution, in 1789. The Hall is open from Easter to October on Saturday and Sunday afternoons only (telephone: 01772 861082).

Whitewell
The Inn at Whitewell

Whitewell nestles between the steep valley side and the river Hodder at the upper end of the Hodder gorge. Although it does boast a road sign, unless you have decided to stop at the Inn, Whitewell has come and gone before you have noticed it. The spacious and attractive Inn at Whitewell was created out of Victorian (dated 1847) additions to buildings which have stood on this spot since the Keeper of the Forest of Bowland was based here in the Middle Ages. The creeper-clad walls and the surrounding woods make this a sublime spot.

The hotel – for that is what it really is – is a large one and has been in its present ownership for many years. Inside there are many prints and antiques and it is unique in having its own art gallery. You will certainly want to look around. The Inn's reputation is very high indeed and it has won innumerable awards for its cooking and its wines. Food is available daily between 12 noon and 2 pm and from 7.30 pm to 9.30 pm. The à la carte evening menu will require you to have had your walk earlier in the day, without doubt an option worth seriously considering for the local Bowland lamb or Goosnargh duck. The bar menus vary from lunchtime to evening so you will need to come during the day if you want my own favourite of warm salad of black pudding. Sweets are home-made and the Inn's pride in its range of cheeses is fully justified. Sandwiches come large and with a salad garnish. Children's portions are available and the vegetarian selection is good. Bar hours are 11 am to 11 pm daily (10.30 pm on Sundays). The Inn is a freehouse with bitters from Marston's, Boddingtons and Bentleys, and Chester's Mild; the stout is Guinness and the cider Scrumpy Jack. There is a pleasant beer garden and dogs are welcomed.

Telephone: 01200 448222. Accommodation is available.

How to get there: From the Trough of Bowland or Slaidburn turn south towards Clitheroe at Dunsop Bridge; from Clitheroe use the B6243 and then turn through Bashall Eaves and past Browsholme Hall. The Inn and church are together beside the river.

Parking: Outside the Inn along a substantial road diversion.

Length of the walk: 1½ miles. Map: OS Landranger sheet 103 Blackburn and Burnley (inn GR 659468).

A steep climb and descent on this short walk are rewarded by the very fine views of the Bowland area. The tiny hamlet of Whitewell has historic interest and is well worth exploring.

The Walk
Note: Great care should be taken in wet or icy conditions.

From the hotel turn next door to St Michael's church. This is a Georgian building which replaced the previous medieval chapel. The son of the house at the Inn found a Bronze Age food preparation mortar in the bed of the river Hodder in 1984 and this is now on display in the church. There is a short path down through the farm to the river bank. Return to the church to start the walk.

On leaving the church, cross over the road and take one of the two roads opposite the Inn up the bank. Immediately at the top is the tiny black and white village hall. Bear left up the lane and pass the drive entrance to the row of cottages, then look for the steps to

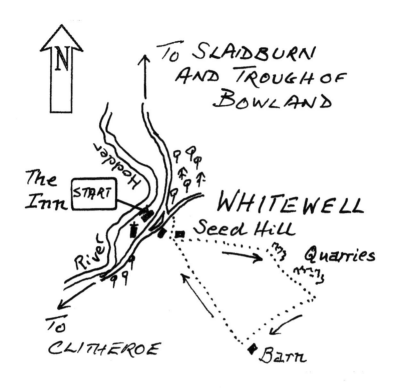

the footpath to the right at the near end of the row of copper beech trees. Cross the field and join the track to swing round the far side of the house, called Seed Hill. Just on the right is the tunnel entrance which gives access for maintenance of the aqueduct which runs through here.

Bear up left along a line of old ash, thorn and holly with indications of a former track. You climb up steadily to a steel gate. The view begins to open up half-left to Whitendale, above Dunsop Bridge, and the Trough of Bowland to its left. To your immediate left is a beech and oak wood on a knoll, bursting with bluebells in late spring. Climb steadily on a green track towards the old quarry and turn slowly right and up through the gap, keeping to the downside of the broken wall, which surrounds a further quarry. The ground flattens off and Pendle Hill comes into view half-left, with Longridge Fell and Parlick away to the right. About 200 yards

A field barn.

short of the road, turn at right angles to the steel gate in the corner of the fence.

On the far side, follow the track down the fence line to the right of the large barn. Up on these breezy pastures oystercatchers, curlews and lapwings call. At the iron kissing-gate in the corner turn to the right on the nearside of the wall and continue on the edge of the pasture to another steel gate in the corner. You have now come round to face back towards Whitewell down below. To the left are the woods of the Hodder gorge, and immediately across the valley at the bottom of the slope is the medieval cow ranch – vaccary – of New Laund (in the woods on the hill slope behind is Fairy Holes cave, inhabited many moons before the Norman barons came to this land – perhaps 2,000 years earlier). Up the valley the double arch of Burholme Bridge should be visible with the isolated cone of Mellor Knoll to its left; to the left again is the wall of Totridge, Whitmore and Fair Oak Fells.

Take great care descending the steep, grassy slope back down to the left of Seed Hill, keeping left of the covered water supply. At one point you are almost looking down the chimneys of the Inn at

Whitewell. Leftwards you should be able to get further views of the valley woodlands. At Seed Hill, return to the path over the field and the steps back to the lane and the Inn.

Places of interest nearby
Down valley, in the Clitheroe direction, is *Browsholme Hall*. Built in 1509, this is the ancestral home of the Parkers – once keepers of the vaccaries around Cow Ark, on the narrow lane between here and Whitewell. The Hall is open to visitors at limited times during the summer months – usually Saturday afternoons, and also at Easter and the two Spring bank holidays (telephone: 01254 846330).

⑧ Slaidburn
The Hark to Bounty Inn

Slaidburn is the capital of the Forest of Bowland and has been so ever since the de Lacys of Clitheroe set up the administration of the Forest here in the 11th century. For hundreds of years it was the only court between Lancaster and York and courts continued to be held in an upper room of the inn until 1937. The warm sandstone of the village buildings make it much of a piece and it is a deservedly popular weekend venue for visitors. The Hark to Bounty (named after a hound) has, itself, been part of the scene since the 13th century and a great deal of the building is low-ceilinged and cosy.

At lunchtimes, food is served between 12 noon and 2 pm, and in the evenings from 6.30 pm to 9 pm (9.30 pm on Friday and Saturday); Sunday service is all day from 12 noon to 8 pm with a special restaurant lunch. The lighter eater is catered for with sandwiches and filled jacket potatoes and salads. Anyone with a hearty appetite will find substantial fare in traditional style – favourites are roast duck, hake and spinach, and baked artichokes. There is a vegetarian choice and children's specials are offered. A

Scottish Courage house, the bar is open between 11 am and 11 pm (10.30 pm on Sundays). In addition to their usual beers there are Theakston Old Peculier, Best Bitter and Mild. Lagers are Foster's, Beck's and McEwans, the cider is Scrumpy Jack and the stout is Guinness. Families are especially welcome and the inn has a children's certificate. There is a small beer garden at the rear. Dogs are not permitted inside during food service times.

Telephone: 01200 446246. Accommodation is available.

How to get there: Use the B6478 either from Clitheroe, to the south, or from Long Preston at the junction of the A682 and the A65, to the north-east; Slaidburn lies at about the halfway point. Alternative minor routes are signed through the Forest of Bowland or from Gisburn.

Parking: There is a moderately sized car park at the pub (please check at the bar before leaving your car while you walk) or use the public car park beside the Hodder bridge.

Length of the walk: 2½ miles, or a short route, round the village only, of 1 mile. Map: OS Landranger sheet 103 Blackburn and Burnley (inn GR 711524).

The short route circuits the village itself. The buildings are extremely attractive and many are of considerable historic interest. The longer option takes you out and a little way up the fellside to open up the fine views.

The Walk
From the doorway of the inn turn left and immediately right to pass the post office and walk out on the Trough of Bowland road. The sandstone terraced cottages here are dated 1820 and are delightful in summer with baskets of flowers. Just beyond, on the right, is a fine horse trough of 1864 and, across the road, Horns Farm, dated 1677. The renovated cottage close by has stone mullions in its upper windows. Look through the gates at the school – the building facing you is the original Brennand's Grammar School of 1717, and is still in use as part of the village school. Enter the churchyard of St Andrew's immediately next door. The building is substantially 15th century but has a font from 1229 and, high on the north wall, beside

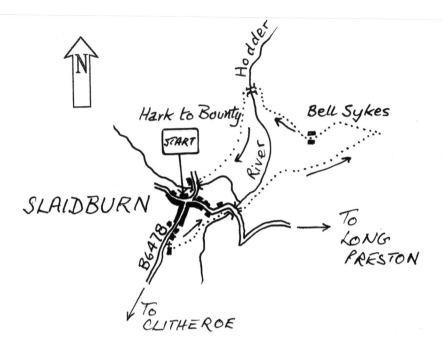

a window, is the stone head of a pre-Christian, Celtic god; there is a Georgian three-decker pulpit and a Jacobean screen. On leaving the church, have a look at the sundial in the south-west corner of the churchyard. Dated 1796, this stands on the site of a medieval cross. Exit from the churchyard at the diagonally opposite corner into the field behind the school through an iron kissing-gate and follow the path half-left across the field to a wooden gate (immediately beside an iron one) onto the riverside path. Go left and join the river bank by an informal car park. This open area by the Hodder is a favourite play area for children.

For the short route, turn left up the brow and return to the inn.

For the main walk, cross over the Hodder bridge, with care for traffic, and take the stone stile immediately to the left, then follow the bank upstream past the junction of the Croasdale Brook on the far side. Walk through a small wood of willow, alder, ash, thorn, sycamore, oak and beech and, at the wall, do NOT use the stile to the left but continue ahead, rising up the bank to a stile over a wire fence. Bear half-right across the field to a wall and a squeeze stile with steps on the far side. Drop to a stone flag over the little beck

Sundial in St Andrew's churchyard.

and continue straight ahead up the slope to a gate in the wall with one limestone gatepost remaining. Bear half-left towards the far corner and a stone stile beside a gate. Follow the faint green track above the runnel on your left to the top right-hand corner of the field and cross the runnel on stones. Hairpin to the left before the gate and take the green track below two large sycamores on a bank, then follow along the left-hand wall. The view is wide open, from the sailing club house on the dam of Stocks Reservoir, to your right, to the Trough of Bowland, far to the left of the wall of fells.

Drop down through a gate into an old track with an avenue of sycamore and ash to Bell Sykes farm. Cross the farmyard and exit on the access track – probably accompanied by peacocks. Continue along the track up the valley to reach an old humpbacked stone bridge over the river. Cross this back to the other bank. Use the track for 150 yards and then branch left on the near side of the wall. After the gate and up-and-over stile, follow the wall to the corner and swing to the right gently beneath the break of slope (do NOT continue ahead on the farm track). Exit to the lane beside Croasdale Bridge. Turn left and go up the brow, past the Jubilee Garden and bear to the right at the war memorial to return to the inn.

9 Tosside
The Dog and Partridge

Tosside village is cut in half by the county boundary so a substantial part of it is not in Lancashire at all (none of it was, of course, until the reorganisation of 1974) but over the border in Yorkshire. The area, today, is significant for the largely coniferous expanse of Gisburn Forest, and the attractions of Stocks Reservoir and nearby Slaidburn. In the 1920s, Tosside was the base for the construction teams for the reservoir and housed between three and four hundred men and their families; all that is now gone. The village pub, the Dog and Partridge, has only been rescued from near oblivion in recent years. The building is tastefully refurbished and, once more, looks an integral part of the scene, both inside and out – it dates from the 1720s originally. It is, reputedly, the highest pub in Lancashire.

Food is served from 12 noon to 1.30 pm and from 7 pm to 8.30 pm every day of the week except Tuesdays. There is a fair variety of choice with the Sunday roast beef and the steaks being especial favourites. An interesting variant on the lighter meal is the range of fillings available with giant Yorkshire puddings. There is a special children's menu and salads and vegetarian meals are on the specials board. The bar opens from 12 noon each day until 3 pm, and again in the evening from 7 pm to 11 pm (10.30 pm on Sundays). A Younger house, the bitter and mild are Theakston, the lager McEwans, with Guinness stout and Strongbow cider. There is a small beer garden at the side of the pub. Dogs, other than guide dogs, should remain outside.

Telephone: 01729 840726.

How to get there: The pub is at the crossroads in the centre of Tosside village on the B6478, which is the road running between Long Preston (A65), Slaidburn and Clitheroe.

Parking: Behind the pub. Please do have a word at the bar before leaving your car while you walk.

Length of the walk: 2½ miles. Map: OS Landranger sheet 103 Blackburn and Burnley (inn GR 769560).

This circuit is mostly within, or at the edge of, Gisburn Forest, where there is a variety of woodland and moorland wildlife to be seen. Much of the route is on good tracks. There are fine views over the eastern Bowland Fells and down the main valley.

The Walk
The church of St Bartholemew and St James (the second dedication arising because the construction of the reservoir drowned the village of Stocks in Bowland) stands next to the pub. It is a simple and unprepossessing building. Behind is the flag-roofed Parochial School. At the crossroads is what appears to be an old drinking fountain, which has been reworked as a memorial to the Queen's Jubilee and which is topped by an interesting weathervane depicting a running fox.

Leave by taking the track – Bailey Lane – on the Slaidburn side of the pub, beside the Forest of Bowland Area of Outstanding Natural Beauty sign. (Note that, despite any evidence you may see to the contrary, this is a right of way as a footpath only.) Walk the length of one field and then continue parallel with the forest boundary on the left. Most of the trees are spruces but there is a

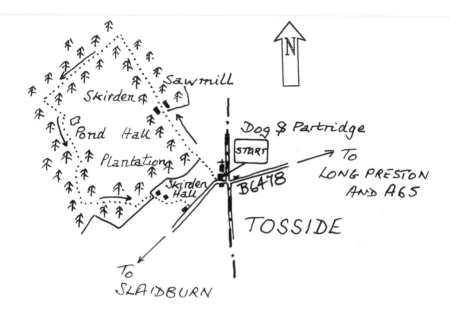

row of attractive whitebeams planted along the edge (the underside of the leaves, as they blow in the wind, will explain the name; the berries are an attractive orange-red in autumn). Pass through the sawmill buildings – beware of moving vehicles during working times. The forest is on both sides now with goat willow growing in the ditches and birdsong in the air. The cry of curlews, lapwings and redshanks from the nearby fields is redolent of upland pastures and moorland. Eventually you reach a Gisburn Forest sign with pine trees on the left.

Bear round to the left 100 yards further on, opposite the entrance to Heath Farm, and stop to admire the views across to White Hill and Bloe Greet and to the south-west, down the main valley of the Hodder. The areas to left and right have been recently cut and re-stocked. This is typical short eared owl country. Drop slowly and, at the bend, go directly ahead on an old grassy track between plantations, with occasional wet patches. Mayflowers bloom on the damp, open, grassy areas in season. Follow through until the ground flattens off and look for the clear, grassed ride, with an old hedge line of hawthorns in the middle of it, to the left. Cross the ditch and walk up to the forest road across from a largish pond.

Running fox weathervane atop the Jubilee Memorial.

Walk to the right along the grey, slatey surface of the forest road and swing round to the left with a stand of Japanese larches on your right (their young twigs stand out red in spring sunshine). The track descends through the forest with alder, willow, thorn and holly beside the old ditches. At the T-junction go left. A few yards further on the footpath goes straight ahead through the trees to cut the bend of the forest road but you may just as well stay on the road itself to cross over a small beck. The route bends right and reaches a field gate at the forest edge. Just before the gate, cross the ditch on the left and walk up the grassy track to emerge by the fence behind Skirden Hall. An old stile crosses the fence in the right-hand corner and the path skirts the garden of the house to join the access track. Continue along this to meet the road beside a house which used to be Sion Chapel (1832) – there is no sign here. Turn left and walk back along the verge for ¼ mile to return to the pub.

10 Halsall
The Saracens Head

The Leeds and Liverpool Canal provides ready access to the flatlands of Lancashire and the pubs beside it. Having served the commercial canal traffic for over 200 years, these now happily supply the leisure users of the canal and the passing trade. The precise age of the Saracens Head is difficult to determine but it, clearly, has stood here by the bridge since the early days of the canal (end to end, building took 46 years from 1770). The scene is particularly attractive on the canalside.

On weekdays, food is served from 12 noon to 2.30 pm and from 5.30 pm to 9 pm; on Saturday it is available all day from noon to 9 pm; on Sundays service finishes at 8 pm. This is an extremely popular venue for folk from miles around and the menu is extensive with an opportunity to mix tastes in unusual ways – steak and scampi, for instance. Main meals are complemented with salads, and there are cold platters and a specific menu for the smaller appetite. Vegetarians and the children are well catered for too. A Tetley house, the bar is open every day from 12 noon to 11 pm

(10.30 pm on Sundays). Beers are Tetley's own, the lagers are Carlsberg and Castlemaine, the stout Guinness and the cider Dry Blackthorn. There is a good range of wines in bottle and on draught. The beer garden is at the side of the canal and adjacent to a particularly good children's play area. Dogs are not permitted on the premises.

Telephone: 01704 084204.

How to get there: From the A5147, Maghull to Southport road, turn for Ormskirk by Halsall church, or from Ormskirk turn for Halsall along Cottage Lane from the roundabout on the A59 at the southern end of the town. The pub stands immediately on the eastern side of the canal bridge ½ mile out of Halsall.

Parking: There is a large car park at the pub.

Length of the walk: 1½ miles. Map: OS Landranger sheet 108 Liverpool (inn GR 375098).

A level walk from a particularly attractive pub location beside the canal. The circuit across the fields from the canal to the village and back by the road includes as pleasant a part of the Lancashire flatlands as you will find.

The Walk

From the front door of the pub turn left and cross the bridge – No 25 – towards the village (take care for traffic, which has no clear sight line over the hump of the arch). Drop down the steps on the far side onto the towpath and turn away from the bridge to walk south. The bridge is a fine sandstone structure and the range of the pub buildings is especially attractive from this viewpoint. Immediately beyond the pub car park is a line of moorings where there are pleasure craft to be seen. Some of these boats are most lovingly decorated in the old style of the canal bargees.

Across to the right, towards the coast, the spire of the church will be in view beyond arable fields – barley, wheat, and cabbage when I last walked through. On the canal, ducks, moorhens and coots quack and chatter and its edges are lined with tall reed grass. The hedgerows are crowded with cow parsley and scrambling vetches and butterflies dance in the summer sun. Away to the left are the

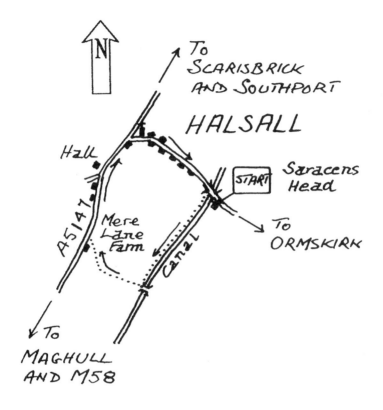

low Clieves Hills, with the square tower of St Michael's church, at Aughton, a landmark for many miles around. Just before bridge No 24 is a barge passing place on the far side. There is a sign for a permissive path up to the right but it is more interesting to go to the bridge itself, where there are grooves worn in the sandstone by the ropes as the horses pulled the barges along. Immediately on the far side of the bridge are steps up to the track above. The view back along the canal through the bridge is lovely.

From the top of the steps turn to the left towards the main road and walk along the track between the fields. Pass the old hawthorn and alder hedge on your left (do not follow the arrow left) and cross to the right of the buildings of Mere Lane farm. Far to your left are the pines on the coastal dunes at Formby. At the A5147 cross with care and walk right along the footway. Immediately to the left are some old brick cottages (more appropriate in this countryside than

Stone canal bridge.

stone) dated 1773. Pass a motor repair shop and enter the Halsall Conservation Area. Cross over the end of Carr Moss Lane. Opposite is the primary school and immediately to your left the finely refurbished Halsall Hall, essentially Georgian in style. As you continue there is an exposure of sandstone in the field over the wall – this explains why Halsall exists, for this must originally have been a dry knoll of land amongst the marshes.

Cross the bridge and go over the road at the war memorial (to the fallen of both World Wars on a much older base) outside the Halsall Arms to the church of St Cuthbert. Although rebuilt in late Victorian times, most of it is much older. Parts of the tower are late 1300s and, interestingly, it begins square, becomes an octagon and then is topped by the spire. Inside are some interesting misericords and an early alabaster effigy on the tomb of a priest. The church will usually be found open on Tuesday and Friday afternoons and at service times. There is a nice sundial in the churchyard. Leave by the path to Summerwood Lane and turn left on the far footway, passing the post office. On the right is a half-moon light over the doorway of a farmhouse. Past the seed merchants the view opens

Renovated Halsall Hall.

up again to the north, with Mill Brow Pumping Station on the skyline; this still keeps the lower-lying land dry enough to farm. A young monkey puzzle tree seems to be doing well in a bungalow garden on the right as you walk along to return to the bridge and the pub.

⑪ Rufford
The Hesketh Arms

Rufford stands where the road comes down off the higher land, which peaks in Parbold Hill to the east, to cross the river Douglas and the main Ormskirk to Preston road, and then snakes away across the formerly marshy plain towards the sea. The Old Hall (and then the New) were, for centuries, the family seats of the Heskeths – hence the name of the elegant Georgian pub, which is a listed building. Built around 1823 it was a coaching house with its own stables and also the court house for the area until the Hesketh estate was sold in 1912.

Food is served at lunchtimes (except Saturdays) between 12 noon and 2 pm. The vegetarian leek, cheese and onion hotpot is especially toothsome, but meat eaters will find Lancashire hotpot (of course!), chicken, sausage and steak, and there are fish dishes plus a specials board. Sandwiches and salads are available, and a children's selection. The dining room serves as a family area. As a Greenalls house, their Bitter, Original and Mild are served. The lager is Carling, the stout Guinness and the cider Scrumpy Jack. Bar times

are 12 noon to 11 pm each day (10.30 pm on Sundays). There is a pleasant beer garden and a shady play area for the children. Please ask at the bar before taking your dog inside the pub.
Telephone: 01704 821716.

How to get there: The pub stands in the middle of the village at the junction of the A59 and the B5246 in the Southport direction.

Parking: There is a large car park at the pub. Please ask before leaving your car there while you walk.

Length of the walk: 1½ miles. Map: OS Landranger sheet 108 Liverpool (inn GR 461155).

Once away from the main road, Rufford is a quiet place and the approach to the superb, historic Old Hall via the canal is extremely attractive. This pleasant circuit is very easily walked. Close by are Mere Sands Wood reserve and Martin Mere wildfowl collection.

The Walk

Cross over the main A59 from the pub with care and take a look back at the frontage of the building. It creates a fine impression and the Victorian additions were well integrated into the whole.

Walk towards the B5246 for Parbold and use the quieter section of the old Liverpool road past the post office and beneath the massive copper-tinged beech tree at Beech House. Turn right on Church Road and pass the Victorian brick and sandstone St Mary's church, built in 1869 to replace a medieval chapel. Pevsner records it in his *Buildings of England* as 'aggressively unattractive' – see what you think. Go over the canal bridge, then cross the road to drop down the ramp onto the towpath and walk north. There are some beautifully kept gardens behind the houses on the far side; in summer swallows hawk over the water for insects, goldfinches twitter in the hedges and ducks dabble in the shade of the overhanging trees. Soon you come parallel with the gardens of Rufford Old Hall and then the Hall itself can be seen through the trees. The mixture of building materials and the surrounding vegetation make for an idyllic scene. Further along, the view opens up and the familiar shape of Parlick, on the edge of the Bowland Fells, stands out. Continue, probably past pensive fishermen, to the swing bridge. The outliers of the West Pennines are visible to the

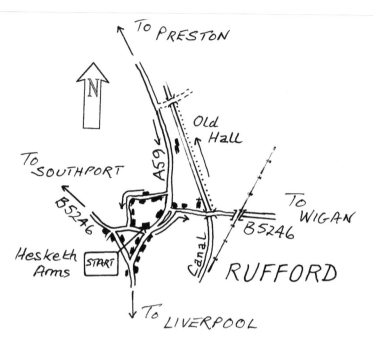

right. Bear to the left over the bridge and walk along the track to the main road, then turn left on the footway to the entrance to the Old Hall.

Rufford Old Hall is a National Trust property, (telephone: 01704 821254) and is open in the afternoon Saturday to Wednesday from April to October. It is one of the outstanding buildings of the North West and is not to be missed. Building seems to have begun in the late 1400s and continued over a long period in a variety of materials and styles which have blended into an intriguing whole today. The brick wing is dated 1662 and the linking section is 1821. Internally, the decoration has the reputation of being among the finest in the whole country. The great hall has a massive hammer-beam roof and a (theoretically) movable carved screen. Arms and armour, 17th-century furniture, a Beauvais tapestry and, in an outhouse, old farmhouse kitchen artefacts, are some of the fascinating treasures here.

Leave the Old Hall by the driveway to the main road and cross to the far footway. Go left beside the sports field and the village hall and turn to the right along Flash Lane (this is one-way traffic in the other direction). There are some pleasant older houses and gardens

Rufford Old Hall.

along the way. Follow the lane round the left-hand bend and notice the re-thatching on the house-cum-stable at The Hermitage. At the T-junction with the Southport road stands the primary school. A sign indicates that you are in the Rufford Park Conservation Area (the New Hall lies behind the wall along Flash Lane); the foundation stones of the former boys' school (1824) and the additional classroom (1850) are built into a modern wall. Return left to the pub.

Places of interest nearby

There are two outstanding conservation sites very close by. Barely a mile along the Southport road is the Lancashire Wildlife Trust reserve of *Mere Sands Wood* (GR 464156) – developed from former sand pits – which has a small visitor centre, various trails and a viewing hide. South-west of the village, and accessed from either the B5246 or the A59, you can cross the moss and find the Wildfowl Trust at *Martin Mere* (telephone: 01704 895181, GR 428143). This gives some impression of what the undrained mosses of south Lancashire must have been like. There are 45 acres of wildfowl gardens and some 350 acres of additional reserve on which in spring and autumn migrating birds can be seen in their thousands.

⑫ Leyland
The Eagle and Child

Leyland was once the capital of the area of Lancashire south of the river Ribble (Leyland Hundred) now served by South Ribble and Chorley Districts. For most of us, today, the name means buses and trucks. The old core remains to the south of the 19th and 20th-century industrial developments and the Eagle and Child forms part of the attractive group of buildings around the parish church. Built in the 1700s (on earlier foundations) the low beams, stone-flagged floor and open fire speak of yesteryear. The pub itself is of interest as the former court house and there are supposed to be secret tunnels to Worden Park, used by the Royalists when escaping from Cromwell's men in the Civil War.

Food is available between 12 noon and 2 pm each day. The menu is focused on the provision of relatively quick snacks and meals. One workers' staple which features is the 'bacon barm' – the barm cake being a flatish, round and unsweetened bun. Because much of the trade comes from people working in the area the protein content of the menu is high – scampi, cod, haddock, steak and kidney, gammon and chicken all feature. This is a Burtonwood pub with their own and guest beers. Lagers are Castlemaine, Carlsberg and Stella Artois, alongside Guinness stout and Strongbow cider. Wine is available too. Bar times are 11.45 am to 11 pm (10.30 pm on Sunday). There is a small beer garden in which your dog will be welcome.

Telephone: 01772 433531.

How to get there: The pub stands close to the traffic lights where the B5254 meets the B5248 – Sandy Lane and Church Road – in the centre of old Leyland, close to the church. The B5256 joins the B5254 from junction 29 of the M6, barely a mile away.

Parking: There is a small pub car park across the road beside the traffic lights and a large, free public car park 100 yards along the road opposite the church.

Length of the walk: 2¼ miles; the addition of the Leyland Cross Heritage Walk would add another mile. Map: OS Landranger sheet 102 Preston and Blackpool (inn GR 541216).

Old Leyland is fascinating historically and this is linked here to the pleasant open space of Worden Park, with its Craft Centre and variety of activities for all the family. Most of the route is on well-surfaced footways or paths and there is a streamside stretch. Nearby historical and transport museums enable you to make a full day out if you wish.

The Walk

Turn left out of the pub door and walk along the footway to the entrance to St Andrew's church. The imposing wall and gateway were erected in 1827. The early 19th-century body of the church links a chancel from the 1300s with a tower built in the 1500s (though a church has been here from Norman times, at least). Return to Church Road and bear left to the staggered crossroads. In the centre of the road is the village cross; the base is original and the fountain and drinking trough celebrate Victoria's Jubilee in 1887. Just around the corner, in Worden Lane, are the 18th-century Clough House (no 7), the Georgian Leyland House (no 10), the new Roman Catholic church of St Mary (1964) and an attractive

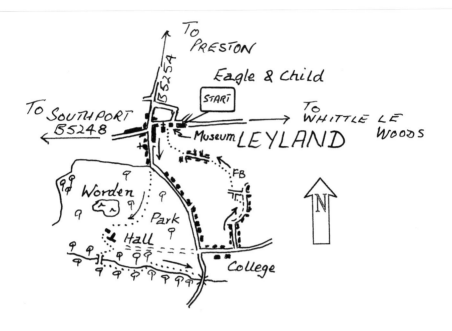

19th-century brick house, The Laurels. Cross over and continue to the gates of Worden Park.

The Farringtons were at Worden and round about from, at least, 1229. The park was taken over by the Council in 1950 and is open from 8 am to 10 pm daily. Much of it is grass with scattered specimen trees. Away to the right is a small lake. Walk ahead towards the former hall site. In this vicinity are miniature golf, a small gauge railway on which you can ride, the Craft Centre (with a variety of working craftsmen), a theatre, and the shop and exhibition centre of the Council for the Protection of Rural England (Lancashire Branch). This latter shows the history of the hall and the Farrington family. The hall was constructed in 1736 but much was destroyed by fire in 1941 and the living quarters demolished in the 1960s. The outbuildings and gardens were renovated in the late 1970s.

Follow the sign for the Formal Gardens and bear left and right for the Arboretum (which is still in a young stage). Walk round the old garden balustrade for a view back to the hall site, the clock tower and the conservatories. Pass a battered old sweet chestnut

Worden Hall Gardens.

and exit through one of the white iron gates to pass the old ice house and drop down to the woods beside the stream. This section may be muddy after rain. Walk upstream, amongst seas of bluebells in spring, to go past the folly arch known as The Ruin and exit onto the Euxton lane at the south-east lodge on the boundary of Chorley District.

Turn left and climb up the brow. The main car entrance to the park, and another car park, are on your left; opposite is Langdale Road. Cross over and walk on the footway past Runshaw College and go left on Cairndale Drive. At the T-junction swing round right beside the grassed area to the footpath sign between the houses to the left. Follow through Nene Close and turn immediately left and right in 5 yards to continue the path between houses and drop through the kissing-gate and over the ditch on an asphalt surfaced path. Rise up again and head half-left with the tower of the church in sight. Join Park Road and continue ahead to the bend at the south-east corner of the churchyard. Turn right and rejoin the flagged walk behind the pub. The small building in the wall is St Andrew's Watch House, of about 1800; this was probably used for bodies awaiting burial.

Places of interest nearby
Just by the pub is the old Grammar School, originally constructed in 1780, and now a *Heritage Museum* and exhibition centre (the *Heritage Trail* starts here, telephone: 01772 422041, and includes some interesting old weavers' cottages and several almshouses). A sign outside directs you to the *British Commercial Vehicle Museum* (telephone: 01772 451011). The collection traces the history of such vehicles back to 1896.

13 Astley Village (Chorley)
The Barons Rest

Astley Village is unusual in being a largely modern, late 20th-century creation – it was to be part of the ill-fated Central Lancashire New Town. It lies next to the western boundary of Astley Park. Despite its name, the pub building is equally modern. The inside is very warm and welcoming and ideally placed for the walk.

The Baron's Table is a substantial menu and offers a considerable list of snacks, including sandwiches, toasties and a good choice of food for children. The home-cooked steak pie is especially popular and goes well with soup of the day. Service times are from 12 noon to 2 pm daily. The bar opens at noon and closes at 11 pm (10.30 pm on Sundays). A Greenalls pub, there are Tetley, Greenalls, Stones and Festival bitters, Caffrey's Irish ale, Murphy's stout and Labbats, Castlemaine and Tennent's Extra lagers; the cider is Scrumpy Jack. There is a pleasant outside patio. Dogs are not permitted on the premises.

Telephone: 01257 277576.

How to get there: Astley Village is to the west of Chorley town centre. Reach it by the A581 for Southport, turning north at the first roundabout and following the signs for the Hall from Westway into the village. The pub entrance is off the public car park in Hall Gate. Alternatively, use the B5252 (Euxton Lane) for Euxton from the A6 and junction 8 of the M61, turning south at the roundabout on the first exit left, Chancery Way.

Parking: There is some parking beside the pub and a large public car park immediately over the way.

Length of the walk: 1½ miles; an optional extension of ½ mile includes the church and town centre. Map: OS Landranger sheet 108 Liverpool (inn GR 574185).

A pleasant walk through Astley Park and some enjoyable woodland with wildflowers and birdlife. The Hall and its art gallery are of exceptional historical interest and the park has a fine children's playground and pets' corner. The additional section of the route allows you to view the remaining older part of Chorley town.

The Walk

The entrance to Astley Park is at the end of the footway behind the shops and signed to the right. Walk past the old farmhouse and swing round beside the former stable block – now a tearoom. Here there is a signboard with a map of the area on it beside the conifers. (My suggestion is that you leave visiting the Hall until last.)

Leave the Hall on your left and bear along the right-hand path and drop down the steps to the right by the bowling greens. Walk round the end and continue right and descend the hill to the stone bridge over the river Chor (from which the town gets its name). Cross over and turn left on the path through the mixed woodland of oak, beech, sycamore and rowan; some of the trees are of substantial size. Up on the right are the open playing fields of Parklands High School. Where the path drops left to the first footbridge continue ahead at the top of the bank and ignore the second footbridge, and the steps to the right (to the school), also. Woodland birds accompany you – particularly wrens and chattering jays – as you keep beside the river now as it ripples over

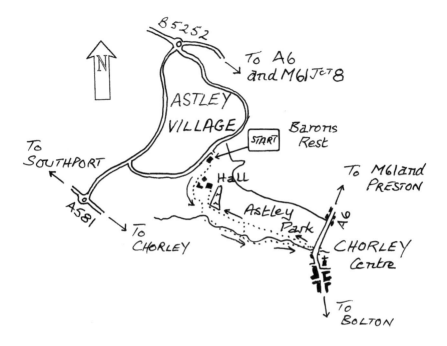

shallows with clumps of soldiers' helmet on its banks. After 300 yards, hairpin back to cross the third footbridge and climb the bank to the right by the wooden post marked 'G' (it is slippy here when wet). You reach the open parkland immediately behind the pets' corner. Turn right and walk around the fence and go up beside the children's play area.

Distance is added if you wish by continuing down the driveway to the main gates – or following the river up to close beside them. Exit to the A6 and cross the road to the fine parish church of St Laurence. Relics of the saint are supposed to have been brought to Chorley by Sir Rowland Standish in 1442. Immediately below the church, down the inclined steps, is an excellent group of Georgian brick houses, including the pub called the Swan with Two Necks.

Return to Astley Village along the main driveway of the park. Note that the park is, in fact, a war memorial dedicated by the town in 1923; a cross stands beside the gate. A Town Trail leaflet is available from the Information Centre or the Council Offices. The open-air market each Tuesday – known as the Flat Iron market –

Astley Hall.

has been in existence since 1498 and is one of Lancashire's largest. It can be found by turning left at the traffic lights uphill from the church.

You may care to wander over the open expanse of grass. In any case, swing left to the Fish Pond dam, beyond the pets' corner and cross over. Turn right for a magnificent view of the glass-filled façade of the Hall – not quite symmetrical. The Charnock family are supposed to have made this their principal residence from the late 16th century. Buildings of this period are best seen from the courtyard. The façade is of the 1650s. Round the entrance hall are some intriguing portraits of famous men – well, famous to Thomas Charnock in the 1640s (many will be unknown to most visitors today). The drawing room has an intricately moulded plaster ceiling and a 17th-century Flemish tapestry of the story of Jason and the Golden Fleece. In the Long Gallery is a shovel-board table (an early variant on shove ha'penny) which is 17½ ft long. An art gallery was added in 1924 and still shows touring exhibitions which are changed regularly. Astley Hall is open daily from April to September (telephone: 01257 262166).

When you can drag yourself away, retrace your steps to the pub from the signboard by the tearoom.

14 Hoghton
The Boars Head

In so far as Hoghton has an identifiable centre the grouping of houses around the Boars Head is it. As you pass by, along the main Preston-Bolton road via Walton le Dale, the church, the village hall and the pub are all that stand out. The building of the Boars Head seems to be undated, but its pleasant sandstone has greeted the traveller for many a year and its low-beamed interior suggests that the façade may well be a Georgian or Victorian addition.

This is a Brewers Fayre pub with a correspondingly extensive menu. As a result, you will find a goodly choice of fish and meats, hot and cold, vegetarian and snacks. I keep looking for things with a local flavour and the minted lamb steaks fit the bill ideally. A farmhouse pâté to start and one of the puddings with custard, from the specials board, would give you a good English meal. Food is served all day, every day, from 12 noon to 8 pm. The bar is open daily from 11.30 am to 11 pm (10.30 pm on Sundays). A Whitbread house, Trophy is complemented by Boddingtons and Whitbread Mild, as well as guest beers. Lagers are Heineken and Stella Artois, the stouts Murphy's and Guinness and the cider Strongbow. An area is set aside for families and there is a non-smoking area inside the pub. Benches outside do duty as a beer garden. Dogs are not permitted inside.

Telephone: 01254 852272.

How to get there: The pub stands at the corner of Gibb Lane where it joins the A675, Bolton to Preston road.

Parking: There is some parking in front of the pub and a large overflow car park on the far side of Gibb Lane.

Length of the walk: 3½ miles, 3 miles when the Tower driveway is open. Map: OS Landranger sheet 102 Preston and Blackpool (inn GR 613266).

The route circuits the hill on which Hoghton Tower stands via woodlands and the valley of the river Darwen, out of which it climbs to Riley Green. Hoghton Tower itself is one of Lancashire's most historic and famous houses. The route may be shortened during its opening times.

The Walk
Turn to the left from the door of the pub and go past the garage which sells former military vehicles (some strange oddities are often parked outside). Turn left again along the footway of Chapel Lane and pass the row of stone cottages. On the right is a pond filled with yellow flag in season; just beyond is the old well. Pass a second pond on your right and continue to the railway bridge. The view to the left is of Preston town centre and round to the fells of Bowland with the separate Beacon Fell standing out. Cross over the bridge and take a look at the former Methodist Chapel (1794), graveyard and schoolhouse on the left.

Turn back to the bridge and take the track down the near side. After the first group of trees, the view opens up to the river Darwen winding through Hoghton Bottoms below and the woodlands of the narrows beyond, where alum (used as a mordant for dyes) was once mined. Drop gradually down amongst the trees and pass the farm ruin with its sandstone flag fences. At the bottom, bear to the right past the renovated Higher Mill (now a house) and walk along

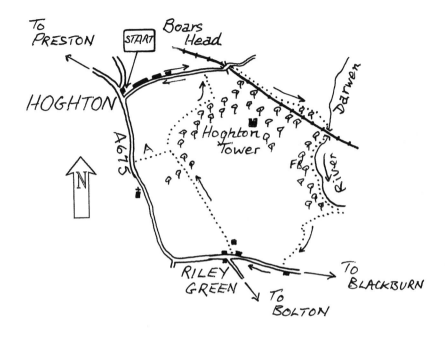

the footpath upriver. You pass through a short, rocky gorge, the railway viaduct towering above, and the river tumbling over rocks full of waterworn potholes below. Up the steep hillside towards the rock on which Hoghton Tower stands are mixed woodlands of oak, elm, sycamore, and hazel; rhododendron provides cover for the pheasants.

Cross a footbridge within the wood and eventually reach an up-and-over stile at the end. The valley ahead has flattened out again and Pleasington stands on the brow up to the left. Turn up immediately right and zig-zag up the slope, following the stony track through the wood and out into fields. At the entrance to Keeper's Cottage there is a kissing-gate. Bear left along the track and take in the view up to the moorland around Darwen Tower; behind you lies the centre of Blackburn. Reach the A6061 almost opposite Newfield and cross with care to turn right along the footway. Recross the road by the car park of the Royal Oak pub (dating from 1711) at Riley Green and walk past the front of it and the notice which announces 'Post horses for hire'. Turn to the right at the end of the building – this used to be the Tower driveway –

Wesleyan Methodist Chapel, 1794.

and walk up to the house of Green farm. Fork to the left along the same line through the fields. There is a good view of Hoghton Tower up to your right; further right still is the unmistakable outline of Pendle Hill. The parish church of Holy Trinity (1824) is down by the main road to your left. Pass through the belts of trees to reach the driveway beside the lodge (1878).

The opening times of the Tower are afternoons on Sundays from Easter to October, Saturdays in July and August and bank holidays (telephone: 01254 852986). Turn up to the right to see where King James I knighted the loin of beef 'Sir loin' when he visited in 1617 shortly after most of the present buildings were completed. Inside are a fine banqueting hall, the state apartments, and exhibitions of documents, dolls' houses, and Chinese teaware.

The route can be shortened during opening times by walking down the drive ('A' on the sketch map) to the main road and turning right along the footway to the pub.

At other times, continue ahead and swing round the field edge beside the park wall past the far cottage. Continue as far as the steel gate in the wire fence and a stile and turn down left on the far side to drop back down to Chapel Lane. Turn left and return to the pub.

⑮ Clitheroe
The Bridge

The town of Clitheroe remains the focus of the central Ribble valley where it has always been relatively easy to cross the river. The Norman, de Lacy, lords made it the seat of a barony and built the castle on the rock which still dominates the town itself. Georgian prosperity left its mark, Victorian industry came and the 20th century has produced its own monument with the massive chimneys of the adjacent cement works. The town is still the focus for the agricultural community for many miles around and is a functional place which, in this case, has retained both history and interest. I should hesitate to guess the number and choice of pubs which serve Clitheroe but the Bridge sits attractively on the built-up edge, giving a feel of the variety of the town without being wholly swallowed up by it.

Food is served all day, every day, from 12 noon to 8 pm. The menu caters for the passing trade with many quick snacks (the children will love it!). Burgers, pizza, kebabs, hot dogs and fried chicken are there among other popular choices. A Whitbread house, the bitters are Trophy, Boddingtons and Flowers, and the mild is Whitbread's own. Stout is Guinness, the lagers Stella Artois and Heineken and the cider Scrumpy Jack. The bar times are 11.30 am to 11 pm each day (10.30 pm on Sundays). There is a family section inside and a pleasant outside area with tables. Your dog is welcome on a lead.

Telephone: 01200 442961.

How to get there: The pub stands on the eastern side of Pendle Road approximately 100 yards from its junction with the inner bypass, Queensway (the A671).

Parking: Outside the pub (or one of several public car parks in the town).

Length of the walk: 3 miles, including the Salthill Trail; the route can easily be shortened to almost any lesser distance by using the side streets. Map: OS Landranger sheet 103 Blackburn and Burnley (inn GR 746417).

There is something to interest everyone on this fascinating walk which combines the attractive townscape of the older part of Clitheroe, with its castle and museum, and the quite unique Salthill Geology Trail. All the route, except the trail, is on footways and you can adjust its length in a variety of ways to suit the time you have available.

The Walk

Leave the pub to the right and cross Taylor Street, then go in front of the tastefully integrated modern Shawbridge Court and turn right along the A671, here called Waterloo Road. The Tesco supermarket has replaced some of the older industrial properties on the far side of the road; just to your right the Mearley Brook is hemmed in by factory buildings. Continue ahead for 300 yards and cross into Salthill Road, with the Royal Oak on the corner, and walk up the brow. You quickly move into much more recent housing beyond Salthill Terrace (1880) and reach a cul-de-sac sign. Walk directly ahead on the track by the limestone wall and pass the Army Cadet barn. Across the grassy area, next to the children's play area, a fine view across to Pendle Hill opens to your right. An

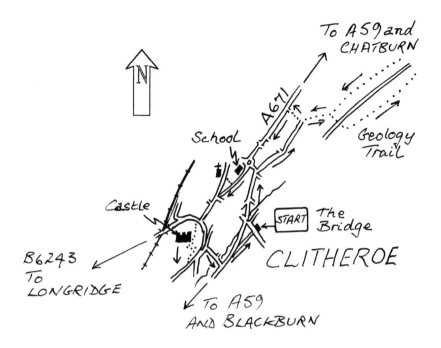

information sign for the Salthill Trail has been erected here by the Lancashire Wildlife Trust. Return from this point if you do not wish to include the trail.

Take the right-hand path through the low scrub and drop down to cross Lincoln Way – the industrial units occupying the bottom of the old quarry will be very obvious. Beside the road are some wonderful rocks full of fossil crinoids (sea lilies). Cross the road and follow the trail along above the old quarry face; the rocks are rich in fossils. (A leaflet is available free from the Castle Museum or the Information Centre and explains the details.) Drop down and cross back over the road at the far end. The trail now goes along the bottom of the quarry face and behind the industrial units; the rocks are filled with crinoids again.

Return to the signboard and go back down to the cul-de-sac sign. Now turn immediately right along the lane behind the houses, a field to your right, and walk through to the main road; now Chatburn Road. Turn left and head for the town centre past the cricket ground on the right. At the roundabout (where the B6478

Victoria Jubilee Memorial in the Castle gardens.

joins) continue straight ahead up York Street. On the right are the sixth form buildings of Clitheroe Royal Grammar School. Almost immediately you step back amongst fine Georgian buildings – or good imitations of them.

Look for the bus stops on the right and turn up the steps and cobbles just beyond to climb up beside the church halls (former schools) to Church Street; half-right is the parish church of St Mary Magdalene. This is a rebuilding of 1829 on the remains of a medieval church. Its spire has dominated the view of this end of the town as you have approached and neatly complements the castle at the other end. Leave the church and head for the town centre past a fine George III building of 1808 (now a solicitor's). You drop a little to the fork in the roads by the Town Hall and the Library; the corner building only dates from 1900 but fits perfectly. Continue ahead up the main Castle Street. To the left is the imposing Swan and Royal Hotel of 1840; other buildings make a pleasing view in either direction.

At the top of the street pass the war memorial (1920) and enter the gardens around the castle. Within these is a tower brought from the Houses of Parliament in the 1930s. Use the left-hand driveway to reach the castle itself and the museum – the much-altered site of the small castle keep. The exhibitions deal with the history and geology of the area. Leave the castle by the steps into the gardens to the right of the door – there is a nice view back from the Victoria Jubilee monument on the first terrace. Drop again and descend to the gate onto Woone Lane and go left and over Moor Lane by the Brown Cow pub. Walk into Lowergate and turn right down Highfield Road; the early industrial Wilkin Square on the left is interesting. Cross Wilkin bridge, then head down to the junction and go left along Queensway. Cross the road and fork into the dead-end on the right along Peel Street to emerge almost opposite the pub.

16 Salterforth
The Anchor Inn

Salterforth lies almost at the high point of the Leeds and Liverpool Canal where it crosses from Lancashire into Yorkshire. The broad valley opens eastwards towards the limestone area of Craven, and nearby Barnoldswick and Earby are the tail-end of the former mill towns on this side of the Pennines. The upgraded B road cuts through the western edge of the village and the Anchor Inn, beside the canal, is now more divorced from the rest of the village than in the past. Probably built about 1655 it originally served the packhorse route from White Moor and over to Yorkshire. Then it catered for the canal trade and now it continues to serve locals and the passing motorist and pleasure cruiser. The present fine stone building was erected on top of the old to raise it up to canal level. Its low-ceilinged cosiness is most welcoming.

Food service times are from 12 noon to 2 pm and between 7 pm and 9 pm each day. Sandwiches, snacks and salads complement a good menu in which the words 'home-made' feature prominently, and folk particularly come to eat here for the genuine chips.

Appropriately, there is a fine selection of filled, king-size, Yorkshire puddings. This is one of those rare pubs which serves that magnificent delicacy cheese and onion pie. A freehouse, Bass, Worthington and Theakston Bitters and Bass Mild are offered, together with Caffrey's Irish ale. Lagers are Tennent's and Carling, the stout is Guinness and the cider both Strongbow and Woodpecker. Bar times are 12 noon to 11 pm (10.30 pm on Sundays). There is a sunny patio area with tables outside and a play area for the children beside the car park. Dogs are not permitted inside.

Telephone: 01282 813186.

How to get there: From the A59 use the B6251 through Barnoldswick and then take the B6383. From the A56 turn onto the B6383 at Kelbrook. Go west at the village crossroads. The pub is 100 yards up the road beside the canal bridge.

Parking: At the pub.

Length of the walk: 2½ miles. Map: OS Landranger sheet 103 Blackburn and Burnley (inn GR 888453).

The route is at first flat, along the canal, and then climbs quickly over the hill and through a country park, with extensive views, to reach the Bancroft Mill Museum, which boasts a working engine. The return is across fields.

The Walk
Cross over the lane from the pub door and walk into the car park area for those using the canal moorings, then join the towpath in the Barnoldswick direction. The canal took 46 years to complete the 127½ miles from Liverpool to Leeds. One of the most impressive engineering feats in its construction lies a mile or two away at Foulridge where a tunnel, just under a mile long, was built, about half of it by making a cutting, building the tunnel, and then back-filling it. Pass the boat moorings and some nice larches and head for the road bridge. In the summer, roses tumble about the hedges and families of ducklings cheep along behind mother. Shortly you reach the demolished bridge of the Barnoldswick railway branch line and then the stone arch of Cockshott Bridge,

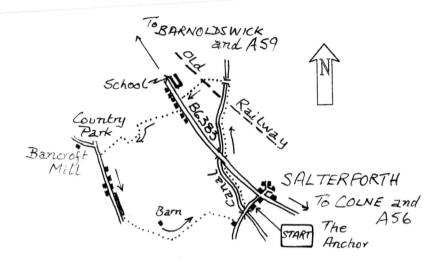

before the marina. Climb up from the towpath here and turn over the bridge to head towards the school along part of the Pendle Way. Bear left at the surfaced track and go left again along the verge at the B6383 as far as the entrance to Lower Park farm.

Cross over with care and find the field gate between houses called Fishcliffe and Parklands. Go up the brow to a steel gate and then bear half-right across the field to a squeeze stile in the stone wall which takes you into the rear of the Cliffe Country Park. The view, through 180 degrees from north-east to south-west, is a fine one; from the Yorkshire Dales, through Kelbrook Moor across the valley, to the Rossendale hills beyond Burnley. The path has been diverted left around the playing areas and a small plantation but eventually reaches the access road (up to the right are the picnic areas). Follow the access downhill to the B6251. At the junction you can see a mill chimney to the right. Go right for 200 yards and then left a further 200 yards to reach the Bancroft Mill Museum on Gillians Lane. One of the last of the mills to come into production, it still has a working engine with a flywheel 16 ft in diameter and weighing 30 tons. The mill is open to view most Saturdays and in the afternoon on the special days when the engine is actually run (check by telephoning: 01282 813751). Return to the country park entrance.

Reflections in the canal.

Continue up the hill with care for traffic and pass the bridleway left, Flattens, the postbox and the bus stop by the stone terrace to a footpath by the last house on the left. Bear left down the faint green track. Look for the steel gate beside the breeze-block barn just below and continue to the small steel gate by the wall corner. The view across the valley is again a fine one; the houses clustered across the other side are Earby. Head across the field diagonally to the right to a stone stile to the right of the stone barn between the trees. Drop left down the wall line and find a squeeze stile at the bottom, then go to the left of the small building housing a water ram pump. Cross the next field to a stile beside the steel gate and turn right along the track past the house called Bashfield Cottage and at the lane (there is no sign) turn left for 200 yards to reach the pub. If you didn't do it before, you will want to hang over the bridge parapet and idly watch the waterfowl and the traffic on the canal.

Places of interest nearby
You could also visit *Earby*, where you will find a Mines Museum in the old grammar school. It would be wise to check the opening times (telephone: 01282 843210).

⑰ Wycoller
The Herders Inn

The Herders is isolated on the edge of the moor on top of which the county boundary runs. Before it became an inn, in 1860, handloom weavers lived here and, no doubt, others before that. The stone frontage along the road was built in the late 1700s. It formed part of the Wycoller Estate before it was broken up and was naturally linked to that hamlet when communication was only on foot or by horse.

On weekdays and Saturdays, food is served from 11.30 am to 2.30 pm and from 7 pm to 10.30 pm; on Sundays (and Saturdays in the summer) service is all day from 12 noon to 10 pm. The inn is famous for its steak and kidney pie and that stomach-hugging delicacy, jam roly-poly. The menu is a comprehensive one so the less hungry, vegetarians and the children will all find a choice. A freehouse, the bitters are John Smith's and Morland Old Speckled Hen, the mild Courage Chestnut. Lagers are Hofmeister and Carlsberg, the stout Beamish and the cider Strongbow. Wines are also available. Bar times are 11.30 am to 3 pm and 7 pm to 11 pm

(10.30 pm on Sundays). The beer garden has a magnificent view across to Boulsworth Hill. There is a family area inside and you are welcome to consume your own food with a drinks purchase. Dogs are welcome on the lead.

Telephone: 01282 863443.

How to get there: **N.B.** The pub is not in Wycoller itself and cannot be reached by car through the hamlet. Use the A6068, Colne to Keighley road, and turn south at Laneshaw Bridge for Haworth. The pub is approximately 2 miles along on the right.

Parking: There is a large car park at the pub, but please ask at the bar before leaving your car while you walk. Alternatively, you can use the Wycoller Country Park car park about ½ mile back towards Laneshaw Bridge.

Length of the walk: 2½ miles. Map: OS Landranger sheet 103 Blackburn and Burnley (inn GR 946390).

Wycoller is an outstanding mill hamlet which has been restored in recent times. There are links with the Brontës, and these can be explored in the fascinating information centre. The walk drops down the north side of the valley and then returns by a higher route, just above Foster's Leap. Some ups and downs so adequate footwear is needed and extra care should be taken in places.

The Walk
Head towards Yorkshire from the door and walk to the corner where there is a small car pull-off. A footpath descends to a stile in the corner of the wall below. Zig-zag down left a little on an old green track and join the farm access track and turn right. Use the wicket gate on the left by the second cottage at Higher Key Stiles and follow the white painted arrows along the wall at the top of the slope round the garden, then join the obvious path along the slope down the valley. The path wanders among old quarry spoil heaps with rushes in a very wet patch. Down to the left you will see the isolated farm of Parson Lee across Smithy Clough. Beyond the notice which says 'private road' drop to the left by the telegraph pole and join the metalled access track, then go over the cattle grid just left of the little wood. There is a squeeze stile to the right just

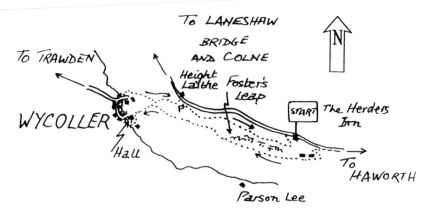

opposite the first house. Cross the field and use two up-and-over stiles and, at the signed path junction, continue ahead on the arrow.

Just beyond this point you come to the first vaccary wall – a series of flagstones set on end to serve as a fence around medieval cattle ranches. Reach a stile where a fence from the left meets a wall. At the stile and gate on the far side of the next field turn left down the broad green track, once a main entrance to Wycoller. Follow this down to the toilet block beside the picnic site at the top end of the hamlet. Turn to the right. There is now an Information Centre – with permanent exhibits about sheep and the woollen industry – a Craft Centre, and an Education Centre in Pepper Hill barn (at the far end). Plenty of information is available about Wycoller and its surroundings as well as its history and links with the Brontës (the Brontë Way – from Gawthorpe to Haworth runs through). The ruins of Wycoller Hall have been made safe and the old cottages and houses have all been renovated and are lived in once more. The clapper bridge and packhorse bridge are very picturesque; it is a delightful spot for children to play by the river.

Browse your way through the hamlet at a gentle pace and turn right over the bridge at the far end (where the lane comes down from the Trawden car park up to the left). Go up left – not towards the Education Centre – opposite the holiday cottage gate and find an up-and-over stile in the wall above. On the far side, aim to the right of the massive stone gatepost with the hole in it and past a second post to meet the track you earlier walked down at the gate opposite the one you came through; this time, turn up to the left. Follow up the steepish slope around the dog-leg to reach the lane

A vaccary wall.

opposite Height Laithe, immediately to the right is the Country Park car park.

Turn into the car park and make for the bottom left-hand corner where you will find a permissive section of path which leads over the bank and along the slope to the third stone fence and an arrowed post. Bear half-left gently up the slope. Gradually move up the contours to an up-and-over stile. Cross over the metalled access track and immediately rise up to the left of the jumbled mass of rocks around Foster's Leap. This is a distinctive pair of large rocks between which it is, certainly, a redoubtable leap! The view between to Boulsworth Hill is dramatic. The path now continues along the top of the old quarry face, with the wall on your left. **N.B.** Particular care is needed here, especially when the grass is wet, and always for young families. Eventually the path drops sharply down to a stone stile to the left over the wall. On the far side, angle up left of the barn in the field corner and pass through two wicket gates to return into the corner of the pub car park.

⑱ Habergham Eaves
The George IV

Habergham Eaves (the dwellings on the edge of the hill) has slowly been subsumed into a steadily extending Burnley. In more recent times, some of the older properties have, in their turn, been knocked down and this part of the Padiham road, known as Cheapside, has opened out again. The George IV – appropriately in the Georgian style of the early 1800s – occupies a corner plot with its unfussy façade. The interior is straightforward too and caters for locals and travellers in a homely way. The fact that it was originally the Farmers Arms suggests traditions around here haven't changed a great deal down the years.

Food service times are between 12 noon and 2 pm, but they do advertise an 'all day breakfast'. Sandwiches, toasties and filled T-cakes (so they describe them) enable a wide choice, for vegetarians and children too. Hot meals are combinations of egg, ham, sausage and chips. The bar is open from 11 am to 11 pm (10.30 pm on Sundays). This is a freehouse and stocks Marston's Pedigree, Higsons Bitter, Boddingtons Bitter and Whitbread Trophy, together with Chester's Mild. Stouts are Murphy's and Guinness, the lager is Heineken and the cider Strongbow. Wine is available on tap. There is a beer garden. Dogs are not permitted inside during food service hours.

Telephone: 01282 771436.

How to get there: The pub stands at the junction of the A671, Burnley to Padiham road, and the A646 (Kiddraw Lane), beside the traffic lights and across from the church. **Note** that no road signs indicate that you are in Habergham.

Parking: At the pub, but please ask before leaving your car while you go for a walk. Alternatively, there is parking at Gawthorpe Hall.

Length of the walk: The full circuit is 4 miles, but you can opt for a much shorter walk to Gawthorpe Hall and back – 1 mile if you use the Habergham Drive in both directions or 1½ miles if you start by using the footway along the A671 between the pub and the entrance to the Hall. Map: OS Landranger sheet 103 Blackburn and Burnley (inn GR 819334).

Gawthorpe Hall (NT), with its collections and gardens, is a fine place to visit. The full walk circuits the Calder valley, largely over fields, with good views and some pleasant woodland. Each of the shortened routes is very easy indeed and requires no more than ordinary footwear.

The Walk

For the shortened routes, either turn immediately left along the footway to link up with the walk at the entrance to Gawthorpe Hall or, if you are using the Habergham Drive in both directions, turn right and then go left just beyond the church, so starting by reversing the final part of the circuit.

For the full walk, cross from the pub by the lights to the church and go right along the footway. Pass the lodge at the end of the Habergham Drive entrance to Gawthorpe Hall and the pink granite drinking trough dated 1859. Bear to the left on the footpath behind the school and between wide-set fences. At the metalled lane at the top, cross straight over onto the farm access track for Top o' th' Close. Bear to the right through the farmyard and take the two stiles into the field. Turn immediately left around the back

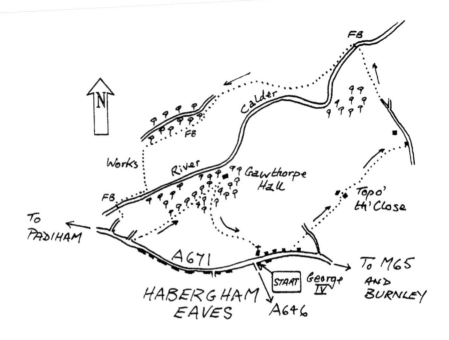

of the barns and go to the track, following this forward under the power lines. After the second stile, continue ahead on the footpath (not the track) beside the right-hand boundary. Walk over two fields – with a fine view up the valley to Burnley and beyond – to exit onto a lane beside cottage gardens. You are now in Ightenhill.

Turn left down the lane and pass Hollins farm on the left. Go back under the power lines. Ignore the footpath sign to the right and keep left (right is the entrance to Hunters Oak). The track becomes a path at the field stile and the Woodland Trust property, Hagg Wood, is signed to the left. Continue ahead down the field – the path is a little uneven under foot here and there – to a steel footbridge over the river Calder. To this point you have been following the Brontë Way; leave it here and pick up the Burnley Way.

Go left down the river bank. Very quickly you join a track. Continue over the cattle grid and walk along the flat valley bottom between the fields. The spire of the church is now up to your left. At Brookfoot, Gawthorpe Hall is in sight over the river amongst the trees. Turn off the access road on the footpath to the left amongst the mixed broadleaved trees and cross the footbridge.

Gawthorpe Hall.

Keep to the bottom path in the wood and bear to the left at the far end, taking the path between the works fence and the field. At the river bank turn to the right and continue to the steel footbridge and recross the river. Walk across the mown grass area to River Drive and go 100 yards right to the main road and left a further 50 yards to the entrance lodge of Gawthorpe Hall at South Drive.

Walk in along the driveway through an avenue of lime trees and into the woodland and gardens around the house; the car park is on the left. This is a National Trust property and is open in the afternoons (except Monday and Friday) between April and October. (telephone: 01282 778511). The gardens (free entry) are open all year, every day between 10 am and 6 pm.

To continue the walk, return to the car park area and turn to the left to find the large gateway of the Habergham Drive. This is slowly becoming overgrown, mostly with alder and willow. Partway along, the view opens to the left to Pendle Hill and the village of Higham. Just before reaching the lodge, turn right into the churchyard of All Saints and St John the Baptist (1849), the spire of which has been overseeing much of your route. Exit the churchyard back across the road to the pub.

19 Haslingden Grane
The Holden Arms

The small communities to the west of Haslingden are hard for the visitor to distinguish, one from the other. Three Lane Ends appears on some maps as Holden Wood but the whole valley has come to be known as Haslingden Grane and the route over the moor as the Grane Road. Without doubt the Holden Arms served the carriers making their way over the moor throughout Victoria's days – though its age is hard to tell. The old photographs displayed on its walls show how things used to be and the location of the former stables is still quite clear. Its nicely appointed and low-ceilinged interior has a comfortable feel about it.

On weekdays food is available between 12 noon and 2.30 pm and from 5.30 pm to 10 pm (9.30 pm on Monday and Tuesday). On Saturdays the times are from 12 noon to 10 pm and on Sundays service ends at 9.30 pm. The menu is a very good one with fish, poultry, meat and salad selections and a fascinating vegetarian variation on the beef Wellington. Starters and desserts are equally varied. A wide choice of teas and coffees is available as well as a separate bar snacks menu and children's menu. This is a Marston's pub and serves their own Bitter and Pedigree. Stouts are Guinness and Murphy's, lagers Carlsberg, Heineken and Castlemaine and the ciders Woodpecker and Strongbow. There is an extensive wine list. Opening times are 11.30 am to 3 pm and 5 pm to 11 pm Monday to Friday, all day Saturday and 12 noon to 10.30 pm on Sunday. There is a non-smoking area inside the pub and a beer garden beside it. Dogs are not permitted.

Telephone: 01706 228997.

How to get there: Use the B6232 (Grane Road) from Haslingden or Blackburn – via Guide. The pub is at the junction with the B6235 for Helmshore (Three Lane Ends), opposite the cemetery.

Parking: There is a large car park at the pub. Alternative car parking is at the Textile Museums.

Length of the walk: 3 miles, but if you choose just to visit the Textile Museums the direct route up and down the road (along the footway) is 1½ miles. Map: OS Landranger sheet 103 Blackburn and Burnley (inn GR 775225).

The full circuit is a relatively strenuous one but well worth the climb up onto Musbury Heights for the marvellous views. The walk continues through the old stone quarry workings and drops down to Musbury Brook. The return route takes in the Lancashire Textile Museums, at Helmshore, both of great interest and open from April to October. Those who prefer can just walk to the museums and back by road.

The Walk

Start along the lane which leads down the left-hand side of the car park by the cottage. Drop down and cross over the dam of Holden Wood reservoir. The view left is across Rawtenstall to the summit of Cowpe Low. Bear up the short brow to the right and continue through the gate labelled 'Tenements Farm' for a further 120 yards; down to the right is the dam of Ogden reservoir (the middle one in the series, Calf Hey, at the top, is out of sight round the corner). Take the well-signed up-and-over stile to the left and go round the field boundary on the right to the top corner (here there is a very

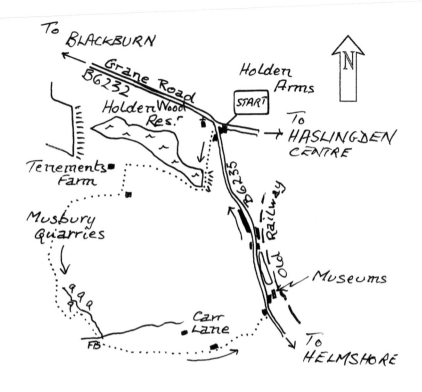

wet patch) to another up-and-over stile below the house. Turn right along the gently raked path which steadily climbs the hillside – this is an old tramway incline for the quarries – beside the broken wall (again there are wet patches) to reach an isolated fence post. The view extends across the valley to Haslingden Moor and Thirteen Stone Hill.

Continue to where the wall and fence meet, then cross through the wall right and go round a small ruin to a footpath post on the track through the workings of Musbury quarries; a chimney stands 200 yards to your right. From these (and other quarries around) millions of flag stones, kerb stones and paving setts were produced from almost horizontal beds of sandstone. Continue easily straight ahead and wander through the quarry spoil heaps. **Note** that the stones are often loose and that there are small cliffs hidden beneath heather here and there off the path. Parents will need to supervise

Holden Wood reservoir.

their children with care in this area. This section is part of the Rossendale Way. At the far side is a stone stile in the wall. Immediately beyond it, bear half-left to an arrowed post and drop down the valley side past two more posts at the left of a gulley. Across to the right the wall represents the boundary of the former medieval Royal Deer Park. Cross the gulley at the bottom beside a T-junction of broken walls and follow the wall line to an obvious green track leading to a ruin at Hare Clough. Turn left between the walls, drop down to the trees by the stream and bear right.

At the steel gate, take the strangely arranged double stile to go over the fence to the right beside the stream and walk down to the main Musbury Brook, where you cross the footbridge. Work up to the left, avoiding the boggy patches as far as possible, and aim for the ruin in the trees with the distinctive high wall below it. Walk through and cross the wire fence at a broken stile. Immediately take the left fork of the path, aiming towards the spire of Helmshore church and Cowpe Low. Pass the iron and stone kissing-gate and then a wooden gate beside the old farmhouse, with stone drip lintels over its windows, and go straight ahead onto the green track which descends the hillside. The lower section of this is finely pitched with stones and has neatly cut cross drains. At the bottom, exit onto the B6235 beside the Airtours headquarters. Pass the car repair shop and, in 200 yards, cross over to the Textile Museums.

There are actually two mills – Whitaker's and Higher. In the former you can see spinning and in the latter are examples of Hargreave's Spinning Jenny and Arkwright's Water Frame. The museums are open from April to October – not Saturday in April to June (telephone: 01706 226459).

Leave the mills and walk up the footway, past the Robin Hood pub, and the cottages set in the hillside opposite with the chimney in the field above. Beyond the mill pond is the old railway viaduct. Continue by the terrace of houses and the pigeon lofts to return to the pub. The former St Stephen's church, at the far end of the car park, was moved here in 1929 after the reservoirs were finished and the valley was depopulated; it now serves as an antiques centre.

Places of interest nearby
Higher up Haslingden Grane (west) there is a *Visitor Centre*.

20 Entwistle
The Strawbury Duck

Entwistle was a scattered and isolated hill farming community which was linked to the outside world by the coming of the railway in 1848 and the building of the reservoirs in the adjacent valleys. Even today there is no formal motorable link through. The Strawbury Duck (that is the spelling; the sign shows what I think may be a mallard) is as far as you can take the car and stands above the station. In its previous incarnation, as the Station Hotel, it also served as the waiting room. The building is an agglomeration of 300 year old cottage, Victorian pub and a 1981 addition, making a fascinating, if unusual, piece of architecture which is something of a warren, with old beams and flagged floors. The odd name is a combined pun on the nearby town of Bury and the, then, landlord's name (which was Duxbury).

Food is available from 12 noon to 2 pm and 7.30 pm to 10 pm on weekdays (not Monday lunchtimes, except for bank holidays) and all day from 12 noon at weekends (to 9.30 pm on Sundays). The menu is a long one. Local black puddings with brown bread and mustard make a fine starter and you may follow on with roast Strawbury Duck itself. To finish, you might choose Fruits of the Forest – even if most of it around here is really recent plantations! Snack eaters, vegetarians and the children are well catered for. This is a freehouse, which serves Marston's Pedigree, Moorhouse's Pendle Witches, Timothy Taylor Landlord and Boddingtons Bitter. Guinness is the stout, Heineken and Stella Artois the lagers and the cider is Strongbow. Bar hours are 12 noon to 3 pm (except Monday) and 7 pm to 11 pm (10.30 pm on Sunday). There is a non-smoking area, families are more than welcome, and a pleasant beer garden is adjacent. Dogs are not permitted inside.

Telephone: 01204 852013. Accommodation is available.

How to get there: From the south, approach Edgworth village by turning from the A676 or the B6391 and turn for Darwen on Blackburn Road at the crossroads; from the north use Roman Road from Darwen via Blacksnape. By either route, ½ mile north of Edgworth crossroads turn down Hob Lane – signed for Entwistle Station – where Roman Road and Blackburn Road meet. There is the alternative of using the railway, but the current timetable should be carefully checked first – not all services stop here.

Parking: At the pub – please ask before leaving your car while you walk; alternatively, at the picnic areas by the dam at the bottom of Battridge Road off Green Arms Road (B6391).

Length of the walk: 3 miles. Map: OS Landranger sheet 109 Manchester (inn GR 727176).

This fairly gentle walk takes you through woodland at the edge of Wayoh reservoir, where the birdlife is particularly interesting. There are some very attractive views.

The Walk

Start from the beech tree, on its stilt roots, by the old-style red telephone box outside the pub and turn along Overshores Road past Station House and the modern bungalows. Take the right fork of the track and drop down to the end of the Turton and Entwistle dam (the plaque records a completion in 1884 for Bolton Waterworks). Cross over the dam; the view up the reservoir is very

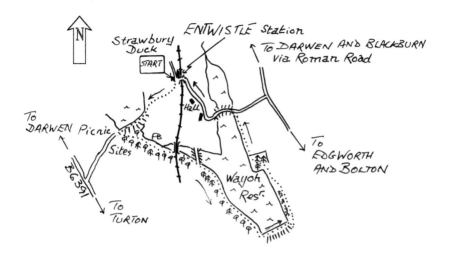

fine, especially in autumn, when the colours of the foliage reflect in the still water. At the far end, turn left through the picnic site at the bottom of Battridge Road; there is an information board here on which you can check your route.

Leave at the bottom left-hand corner, on the concessionary footpath, into mixed broadleaved woodland and follow the arrows amongst large beech and sycamore. The underlying sandstone rock is exposed at the footbridge. Drop under the sandstone and brick railway viaduct high over your head and continue ahead; there is considerable natural regeneration of beech and holly here. Walk forward on the broader path, passing plantations of larch, pine, and spruce beside the Wayoh reservoir. At the bottom of the reservoir, turn left on the metalled road over the dam (with the treatment works way down below on the right and the church on the brow).

On the far side, zig-zag right and left up along the green rails to walk above the quarry face beside the reservoir. House martins hawk for insects over the water surface in summer and heather blooms on the bank here. A variety of waterfowl is to be found on the reservoirs, with migrants passing through in autumn and spring. Walk amongst the heather to the field wall and pass through. The view up valley to Whittlestone Head is a good one and that across the reservoir to the viaduct, under which you walked earlier, is picturesque. Keep to the lower stony path and drop down to reservoir level again. An area of willow carr extends along this side

The giant beech at the start of the walk.

and is a favourite feeding area for mixed flocks of small birds; willow herb and thistles carpet the banks beneath the shaly outcrops and in season there are masses of wild raspberries (if you get there first) by the mixed conifer plantation.

Exit eventually to Entwistle Hall Lane and cross the large culvert to the left, then walk up the steep hill past Higher Crow Trees farm and Entwistle Hall farm on the left. Cross the bridge beside the railway station to reach the pub once more.

Places of interest nearby

Down valley, beside the B6391, is *Turton Tower*. Originally a defensive pele tower, this was modified about 1600 and became a hostel for Parliamentary troops during the Civil War. It was refurbished in Victorian times and then served as offices for the former Turton Council for many years. It is now a Lancashire County museum. Opening times vary (telephone: 01204 852203) but are essentially afternoons. There are interesting collections of furniture and armour and contemporary visiting exhibitions.